Surviving Myself
The Making of a Middleweight

By

Peter Wood

Book Reviews

"Peter Wood's writing is easy to read and hard to put down."

--Benjamin Cheever, author of the Partisan, Editor's Choice of the New York Times Best Books of the Year

"Wood's writing is in John Green territory. Peter throws a sweet sentence and can knock you out with a paragraph."

--Robert Lipsyte, Author of The Contender

"Wood, as a middleweight, hit his opponents on the head with punches; now he hits the reader in the brain with words…his writing is exciting, insightful, and inspiring…"

--Bert Sugar, sports-media icon with his trademark cigar and fedora. Sugar is regarded to be "the greatest boxing writer of the 20th century by the International Veterans Boxing Association.

Table of Contents

Dedicated To

Jane Carroll Wood

Other Books written by Peter Wood

To Swallow a Toad

A Clenched Fist

Confessions of a Fighter

The Boy Who Hit Back

Although this is a memoir, and represents the whole, crazy, objective truth, I am advised of the slim chance that some of the people described in this book might remember things differently. To accommodate this absurd possibility, some of the names have been changed.

The Little Boy

I knew a boy, a little boy
A long, long time ago.
His eyes were bright,
His step was light,
His heart was all aglow.

And though his world
Was young and gay,
A magic carousel,
And all the happy
Games he played
I still recall so well.

There came a time we said goodbye
We've been apart since then,
And no one knows as well as I,
He won't be back again.

And though I search
Around the world until eternity,
I'll never find that little boy
That boy I used to be.

Lyrics by Al Stillman

Music by Guy Wood

Recorded by Tony Bennett

MY EARLY YEARS

A Knife to My Brother's Throat

Circa 1954

I'm not special—but my story is…

When a kid held a knife to my brother's throat in the school bathroom, it altered our family forever—and not for the better…

Our Upper West Side apartment, on the edge of Harlem, is where my parents rub shoulders with famous playwrights—Stephen Sondheim and Arthur Miller—talented actors, Chita Rivera and Zero Mostel, and well-known singers—Barbra Streisand and Liza Minelli, plus a few communists.

My parents—Guy and Nathalie Wood—aren't communists, but they are artists—not nearly as successful as the people I just mentioned. But they are enjoying the liberal lilt of our artistic neighborhood—until this knife thingy.

"I think we should move," says my mother.

"B-But…," stutters my father.

"But *what*?"

"What about my job and all our friends here in the c-city?"

"What's more important than our boys' safety?"

My parents friends include Morton Deutsch, a Columbia University professor and Betty Friedan, an ultra-radical journalist. She isn't famous yet, but, boy, she's gonna be.

Their friends beg them not to move. Professor Deutsch says, "What happened to your son was a random event—it could have happened anywhere."

"That's right," adds Betty Friedan, "crime is everywhere."

But my parents others friends, Tex and Irving Elman, two struggling script writers, didn't listen to them and fled the city and are now enjoying the peaceful suburbs of Rockleigh, New Jersey.

At home, my parents begin screaming at each other, slamming doors, and start avoiding each other. That's what a sharp knife to a boy's throat will do.

"We c-can't always give in to our fears," stammers my father.

"Guy, it's better to be safe than sorry."

"We *can't* leave," says dad.

"We *must* leave," says mom.

We leave.

Closter, New Jersey

Before I tell you how I got a little messed up, I need to give you some important background information…

We're now living in a cute Dutch cottage with a sloping roof, and a Dutch door which opens on the top and the bottom. This cottage is nestled between privet hedges and a gravel driveway runs along the left side (that leads to a small opening on the side for milk deliveries from Dellwood Dairy.) On the right side is a screened-in porch with a flagstone floor. In late August we can sit on the porch and smell the wild grape vines perfuming the air. In the backyard is a small goldfish pond.

"Blimey! I can walk to the bus stop!" says my father. Dad still uses weird words like *blimey, bloke,* and *cheerio* because he's from Manchester, England and emigrated to America in the 1930s.

Each morning dad drinks a cup of Tetley with a *spot* of milk, then hops onto the #84 Red & Tan to George Washington Bridge in Fort Lee. He then grabs the "A" train at The Port Authority which brings him to Tiny Pan Alley in the Brill Building, next to Jack Dempsey's Restaurant on Broadway.

Closter is an idyllic hamlet with more fresh air and open space than the Upper West Side—and there are no third-grade punks packing sharp knives.

My mother now joins the PTA and becomes a suburban housewife. She shops at A&P, cooks our meals. And makes our beds. She is happy. But she's still in her mid-twenties, a former Ford model, and I *now know* she was afraid to ask herself a dangerous question—*Am I really happy?*

She stares out the window at our privet hedges and the quiet tree-lined street and secretly transports herself back to the excitement of rubbing shoulders with celebrities in New York City. She asks herself—*Is this all?*

I'm a happy little three-year-old, and much happier than my twenty-seven-year-old mother…

A few years pass and my mom is smiling less and less. Actually, she's falling apart.

A Dying Career

More years pass and Professor Deutsch, my parent's old New York City friend, has already written books and papers on his special topic—peaceful coexistence— *a theory that will be shoved down my throat in the years to come.*

And Betty Friedan, has written a ground-breaking book—*The Feminine Mystique*—and becomes known as *The Mother of the Feminist Movement.*

And Tex and Irving Elman have moved, once again, and are flourishing in the Pacific Palisades in California. They are now writing scripts for the *Alfred Hitchcock* television series.

Unfortunately, my father can't keep pace—his songwriting career is sputtering…gasping…dying.

When Was Your Last Hit Song, Guy?

I'm still young and don't remember my father much. I might recall seeing his back hunched over his piano, but, honestly, I probably don't even remember that. He's too busy on Tin Pan Alley trying to catch a break. But it's the late 1950s and Dad's pop music is out of fashion. The Beatles and Rolling Stones are *in*, and Paul Anka, Annette Funicello, Perry Como, and Bobby Darin, and my dad—are *out*.

Each morning before dad leaves for work, he says to my mom, "When I get home, please have the boys already in b-bed."

I was too young to understand any of this stuff then, but I'm slowly piecing it together now. I was only a toddler, wetting my bed, sucking my thumb, and rubbing the blue satin of my favorite blankie against my cheek—just like Linus, of *Peanuts*.

Tex and Irving Elman continue to flourish in California and we keep getting their postcards: *We're the new head scriptwriters for Search for Tomorrow and General Hospital!* **These** postcards keep coming from Chile, Japan, and Hawaii.

My mother looks up from a postcard and goes, "When was your last hit song, Guy?"

That year my father sold our green Jaguar—a used white Plymouth Valiant now sits in our gravel driveway.

What's Wrong with You?

I'm about four now, sitting under dad's black piano listening to them shouting.

"L-Let me get this right," says my father, "you want to get a job?"

"Yes. I *need* a job," says my mother.

"You *have* a job! The boys are your job!"

"Honey, I'm becoming exactly the kind of woman I always hated."

"What's wrong with you?" he asks.

"I don't know."

"You're not going to take care of the boys anymore?"

"They're older. Peter's in nursery school and David doesn't need me as much."

"They need you now more than ever!"

"Honey, I'm *unhappy*," she cries. "It's a new world today. Women are finding jobs and going to work."

My father looks at the book laying on his piano and holds it up. "Everything's changed since you've read this crap." It's Betty Freidan's *The Feminine Mystique.*

"I have dreams and ambitions of my own," she says. "I want to become a designer---a clothes designer."

"Oh, that's w-wonderful! One minute I'm living with a wife and now you're asking me to live with a clothes designer?"

"It won't be like that," she cries.

"I forbid it!"

That's when Betty Freidan slams to the floor.

An Old Worry-Wart

How can I ever grow up to be strong and tough if I have such a gentle, mild-mannered stutterer for a father—a song-writer who worries about everything?

Dad *chain—worries* the way other men chain—smoke. Worry is as visible as the deep grooves etched on his forehead. You'd think a man with music in his heart wouldn't have a dark cloud hanging over his head all the time.

He's always:

"P-Peter, put on your thermal underwear—it might get cold."

"David, don't drink water during meals, it dilutes your digestive system."

"Peter, chew 20 times before you swallow."

"David, that's too much toilet paper!"

"Nathalie, why buy a newspaper when it's free in the l-library?"

"Oh, no—the stock market..."

"Peter, bring your galoshes, it might rain."

"Peter, I don't want you watching The Three Stooges, it's too v-violent."

"Nathalie, how much did that dress cost?"

"Peter, you're wheezing—rub Vicks-VapoRub on your chest, and put a smear under your nose."

"Nathalie, more red shoes?"

"D-David, I said you're using too much toilet paper!"

Dad's a good father—he's not a mass murderer, or anything. He never curses, drinks, or hits us. But worry is his constant companion. It ruins everything. Why is he so fearful?

I sometimes hear my mother whisper, *Why did I marry such an old worry-wart?*

I Hate You

I see it much clearer now—since we've moved to the suburbs, mom's been gulping down her unhappiness with her morning coffee. But now her unhappiness is spilling over. Her *body* is in Closter, New Jersey, but her *dreams* are back in New York City.

The Feminine Mystique is screaming in mom's ear.

How many women are struggling with this gnawing sense of emptiness and stagnation?

In 1965, Anne Morrow Lindbergh wrote *Gift from the Sea*. Lindbergh describes my mom perfectly with the German word, "*zerrissenheit*— torn-to-pieces-hood." Maybe she's read that book, too. Sure, mom loves her green privet hedges, her goldfish pond, and me and David, but she's still young and pretty and only in her mid-twenties. She's tasted success as a Ford fashion model and now what...*Laundry? Cooking? Cleaning?*

One evening, mom looks up from a frying pan at her older, failing, stuttering husband, and says, "Guy, you can't clip my wings forever."

"Nathalie, I love you," he says. "I want you home with the boys. It's where you belong."

"I *hate* you!" she screams.

Jumping Out a Window

A hysterical woman dressed in a nightgown has jumped out the window of her home and in desperation is running down Closter Dock Road. A policeman spots her and drives her to the Closter police station for psychiatric observation. She's my mom.

The image of my mom crawling out a window and running down the street in her nightgown is a recurring nightmare.

A month later, my father comes home from more failure on Tin Pan Alley, opens the front door, and discovers an empty house. *"Blimey!"* he later told me, "the house was empty. I almost had a heart attack."

You'll have to wait a few more chapters to see how all this stuff kinda effected me.

Our New House on West Street

Well, anyway, me, my mother, and older brother, are now living in a small rental across town. I don't see much of mom because she's working in New York City. And we don't see our dad at all.

Grandma Mary, flew in from Toledo, Ohio, is now taking care of us. Gram's got long white hair, a pleasant laugh, and smiley blue eyes. She says, "Boys, get ready for me! I'm a throwback from the Roaring 1920s—a flapper."

"What's a flapper?" asks David.

"We smoked cigarettes, drank whisky, and danced the jitter bug with our skirts well above our knees." Gram loves reading big fat books of historical fiction, writes beautiful-handwritten letters to her friends back in Ohio, religiously watches Red Skelton and Lucy Ball on television, and chain smokes unfiltered Pall Mall cigarettes. When she coughs, I hear wet stuff rattling in her chest.

Gram also visits the bar in town, sometimes dragging me along.

Our small rental is *the cat's meow*, (that's Gram's expression.) I climb onto the roof from my bedroom window or hide in the coal bin down in the basement. But most of the time I'm exploring the fields behind our house with Stick-o, my imaginary friend—a cowboy with a pearl-handled pistol and palomino horse. We roam the backfields with Ginger, my pet cat. Ginger is a *genius* who—I kid you not—poops in our upstairs toilet. *She's the cat's meow!*

It's a true fact that me and David have all the freedom in the world now because our parents aren't around. But I'm so stupid I don't even realize my father's not living with us…until one Saturday afternoon I see him. He opens the door and steps inside!

"GET OUT!" shrieks my mom.

I'm pretty sure my mom isn't insane, but she starts acting it, pushing and hitting my dad.

"D-Don't hit me, dear," he frowns.

"I'm not your *dear*! Get out!"

My father grabs her shoulders and tosses her to the ground. She bounces up screaming. *"YOU BASTARD!"*

He drives away in his white Valiant and never enters our house again. And that was that.

I know something really really bad bad bad has just happened, but I'm not sure what it was.

That's when me, Stick-o, and Ginger go outside and escape to the backfields.

A Pea-Green *Lawn-Boy*

It's Saturday and my mom is sitting in the living room. She goes, "David, I have something important to tell you. Sit down."

He sits.

"What?"

"David, you are now the man of the house."

"Me?"

"Yes, you."

"Mom, I'm only twelve."

"Yes. And since your father's not here anymore, I expect you to assume added responsibility."

The following weekend, a brand new, pea-green, *Lawn-Boy* is sitting in our driveway. My mother smiles and says, "David, this is yours."

"Why?"

"Because you're the man of the house!"

The man of the house pulls back his shoulders and smiles.

David—My Older Brother

Important background about David:

When David was born at Mount Sinai Morningside Hospital, my mother cried. That tiny colicky thing screaming in the incubator was *hers*. She said, "He looked so pink and helpless. It broke my heart. He never stopped crying. I quarantined him at home and no one entered his nursery without a facemask and gloves. Later, when I took David out for fresh air in Central Park, the other mothers looked in his stroller and saw a crying infant wearing a facemask. They were always polite and told me how cute he was."

David was not a fun baby.

So now David is *the man of the house*. Let's see how long that lasts.

David has quit everything he's ever started—Cub Scouts, Boy Scouts, Little League baseball, piano lessons, and trumpet lessons. Our parents bought him a dog, but that didn't last long, because he hated cleaning up after it.

Honestly, I think a colicky infant is becoming a colicky preteen. That's a true fact.

I've also noticed that David never gets too friendly with work. He hates chores, errands, and tasks. He leaves his dirty dishes in the sink, throws fits when our mother asks him to weed the flowerbeds, and he never makes his bed. Chores suck.

David is five years older than me, and I still kinda idolize him even though he teases me and bosses me around. He's stronger than me, more handsome, and way more intelligent. He's a straight *A* student who doesn't stutter, like me, and he's very charming when he wants to be. I'm even envious of his educated handwriting.

In Village School, he's submitted the same book report on *The Red Badge of Courage* for two straight years. He's figured out all he has

16

to do is add a few uppity words and throw in a few pretentious compound-complex sentences and he gets his *A*.

He's sneaky.

Filthy Smut

Yeah, David loves being *the man of the house*, but he hates mowing the lawn. So he does the most obvious thing—he grabs a hammer and smashes his brand-new pea-green *LawnBoy* to shit.

"Why," cries my mother, "did you do this?"

"Because I hate that thing!" he yells. "And I'm not cutting the lawn anymore!"

"But you're the man of the house! You *have* to!"

"No, I *don't!"* he screams.

"Yes, you do!"

"Make me!" he says, running up the stairs and slamming his bedroom door.

Yeah, a colicky infant is definitely blossoming into a colicky 12-year-old.

I've noticed something weird about my big brother. When he sleeps he tucks his head under his blanket. I'm no psychiatrist, but I think he's trying to crawl back into the dark safety of his mother's stomach—a quiet place where there's no chores, no responsibility, and no pea-green *LawnBoy*.

A week after David hammered his lawnmower to death, my mother found a *Playboy* hidden beneath his bedsheets. The man of the house has been looking at porn! *What's wrong with him? Where has she failed as a mother?* She's Massachusetts' Puritan and disgusting smut will *never, never, never* be tolerated in her house! With disgust, she races downstairs while ripping the evil smut to shreds. She opens the back door, casts out the nastiness, yelling *Sick! Sick! Sick!*

David's evil smut is now scattered all over our backyard for me to find the next morning. I know I shouldn't do it, I just shouldn't do it,

18

but I do it anyway…I pick up the evil smut and, sneak into our garage and discover what an Arabian harem looks like: beautiful naked women with big bosoms and hairy vaginas lying around on colorful Persian rugs with a black man fanning them. I kinda like it.

My Mom

I think my mom is fantastic, I really do. But she's molly-coddling David. Even *I* know that. Maybe she still sees David as a helpless pink thing crying in a hospital incubator and she feels guilty? But if she doesn't stop pampering him, he'll become a victim of her over-parenting.

As I said earlier, David wasn't a fun baby. But now he's becoming a real big pain in the ass.

Me, when I was born at Mount Sinai Morningside Hospital, I was a perfect sweetheart, if I do say so myself. But my mom already had gone through enough bullshit with David, and I bet she thought to herself, *Oh, no! Here comes another headache.*

Me? I'm the beneficiary of my mother's *under*-parenting. But don't get me wrong—that's totally okay. Her inattention to me is a gift because I'm growing up strong and independent—well, that's what I tell myself. As I mentioned earlier, I'm gonna grow up to be a strong man some day.

I now better understand why mom fled the suburbs leaving her two sons in the care of her mother. It isn't *all* Betty Friedan's fault.

My mother wanted to be more than just a mother.

I'm being honest here—my mom is wonderful, and I'm not saying that because I think I should. And she always sees the good in people. She sees the good in David and in me and in all mankind …except for my failing father, an old worrywart.

Gifts from Our Mother

After my mom recuperates from David's evil smut, she returns from New York with a large gray aluminum box and sets it on our kitchen table.

"What's that?" goes David.

"Open it," she smiles.

He unhooks a latch and swings open two folding doors. Inside are rows of small glass vials filled with pretty powders and granules— blue, green, red, pink, orange.

"A chemistry set," smiles my mother.

David is puzzled.

She then hands me a deck of poetry cards. "For you, Peter!"

What does a future tough guy like me do with poetry cards? Well, I go up to my bedroom and arrange Thoreau, Tennyson, Whitman, and Dickinson on the wooden floor. Every face has a beard, except for Emily Dickinson. I end up flipping them against the wall like they were Mantle, Mays, Pepitone, and Minnie Minoso.

It's not much fun.

David never figures out what to do with the pretty powders and granules of his chemistry set. But he has fun pouring Coke on the green granules, striking matches to the blue ones, and feeding our cat the orange ones. In fairness to him, how does a seventh grader use a chemistry set intended for high school chemistry students?

At least he didn't hammer it to shit like his pea-green lawnmower.

Five decades later, when David was 67 year old, while lying on his death bed in the West Palm Beach Hospital, he whispered to me,

"Peter, I think West Street was the time when my life started going downhill."

Dang! He was only 12 years old.

The Emerson Hotel

The Bergen County Family Court has finally granted my mom a divorce. Her old worry-wart ex-husband gets visitation rights every other weekend and every other Friday night. His alimony payment is $35 a week.

*****

Tonight, Dad drives me and David to the Emerson Hotel Steakhouse, famous for it's specialty—thinly sliced steak layered over toast-points with sizzling hot butter and fries.

At the table Dad is quietly looking down at his menu. *What's he thinking? A melody? His failed marriage? His floundering career? Or is he just deciding on the baked potato or French fries?*

All three of us order the house specialty.

When the waiter brings our food, my steak is swimming in a yellow puddle. "There's too much b-butter," I stammer.

"Shut up and eat," says David.

"Please, don't speak to Peter like that," says my father.

"He's a *widdle widdle* baby," teases David.

"Am n-not!"

"Are t-t-too!" he mocks.

Our father is still quietly looking down at the table, not saying anything.

I'm staring at the pool of melted butter on my plate.

"Stop staring at it, dummy," says David.

"There's too much b-butter!"

"Eat it and shut up," he frowns.

Dad seems to have disappeared into himself. *What's he thinking?*

Finally, he looks up and says, "I-I just don't know, boys. It doesn't look like your mother and I will be getting back together…I'm lost." He looks past my shoulder. "The music business isn't going well and I might move to Los Angeles."

My body stiffens and my lips start quivering. The thought of losing my father hits gut level.

He sighs. "Sometimes I think I should just end it all and jump off the Brooklyn Bridge."

Tears stream down my cheeks and my body shakes. I'm such a cry-baby. The rest is all a blurrrrrrrrrrr.

I will never step foot into the Emerson Hotel Steakhouse again.

Waiting for Dad

I'm waiting for dad to pick me up for his weekend visitation. I'm looking out the picture window waiting to see his white Valiant.... *10...9...8...7...6... Dad's coming around the corner...5...4...3...2... right* **now**!...

Dad and I don't have to do anything special, just knowing he's near me is good enough.

I'll probably play wiffle ball with Paul DeKovessey on the front lawn of his Dutch cottage. Paul will be Mickey Mantle and I'll be Minnie Minoso of the Chicago White Sox. Afterwards, Dad will drive us to 7-Eleven for a Slurpee and two Suzie Qs.

...10...9...8...7...6...5...4... Dad's car is coming around the corner...3...2... **right now**!...

David's still upstairs in bed with a blanket over his head. Spending weekends with Dad isn't such a big thing for him. It is for me.

When my dad was my age he met his father once once—He told me: *I was a wee lad in Manchester when my parents divorced. My dad was a Christian and my mum a Jewess. In England, mixed marriages were taboo and it was reported on the front page of* **The Manchester Guardian**. *Well, one afternoon, my dad and I finally met at a park bench in Cotton Field Park. He bought me a meat pie and an Eckles Cake for dessert. We agreed to meet the following week. But he never showed up. He absconded.*

*...10...9...8...7...6... Dad's coming around the corner...5...4...3...2...***DAD!**

When Was Your Last Hit Song?

When dad was younger he cranked out three hit songs which topped the charts: *My One and Only Love, Till Then, and Shoo-Fly-Pie & Apple Pan Dowdy.* But that was *years* ago. Now the *British Invasion* is cranking out rock'roll—The Beatles, The Rolling Stones, The Who, The Kinks, The Animals, Dave Clark 5, Herman's Hermits, Manfred Mann…Songwriters like my dad are squeezed out.

Meanwhile, my parents' friends, Tex and Irving Elman's writing career in California is still flourishing! Their postcards are coming from Chile, Fiji Islands, and Alaska: *We're writing and producing five new television series! "The Eleventh Hour", "Ben Casey", "High Chaparral", and "Slattery's People". Ha! And we're still frugal—traveling on cargo ships!*

…Guy, when was your last hit song?…

Every night before bed I drop to my knees and pray. *Please, God, help my dad. Don't let him jump off the Brooklyn Bridge.*

The Hangman

I love David, but he's nuts. He and his buddy, Joe Kaufman, are goofing around in the backyard, next to the goldfish pond, when he suddenly screams, "Peter, get Dad! Hurry!" I look at Joe dangling from a tree limb—a noose is wrapped around his neck and his legs are kicking wildly.

When Dad opens the back door, Joe's tongue's sticking out and his legs are limp. Words like *bollocks and gob smacked* fly out of dad's mouth.

David starts laughing. "It's a prank, Dad! He not *really* hanging!"

I can't remember if Joe is sent home, or if David, the little rascal, is punished. If he was punished, it wasn't much. Dad's too mild-mannered and my mom is too guilt-ridden to be a strict disciplinarian. When Gram hears about it, she yells, *YOU LITTLE SHIT! WAKE UP AND FLY RIGHT!*

Ginger

Ginger is sitting on the upstairs toilet taking a dump. She's my genius cat I told you about—who doesn't use a litterbox like ordinary cats. She looks up and says, *Peter, something's wrong with your brother, David.*

Why do you say t-that?

Because he ties me up with that clear plastic you get from the cleaners. He ties my legs so I hop around like a baby goat.

Does he hurt you?

No. He's just having fun. Sometimes he tears off long strips and knots them around my tail—like I'm a kite. He enjoys that too.

Why didn't you tell me this before?

Well, David loves me. He's very kind, and at night when I sleep on his bed, he always scoots his legs over to give me room. Sometimes he falls asleep with his feet hanging off the bed.

Tying you up, Ginger, isn't natural.

That's why I say there might be something wrong with him. Does he ever tie you up?

No.

Well, not yet.

I flush her cat pooh down the toilet and watch her pad softly downstairs past David's bedroom.

First Grade

I'm not the tough guy you see on the cover of this book, but give me a chance. I'm still only in first grade, still stuttering, sucking my thumb, and wetting the bed. *That's so embarrassing!*

Well, right now I'm sitting in the back row of Mrs. DeCastro's class because that's where she stuck me. It's probably because I wet the bed last night and she smells my pissy underwear. And what about Todd Munson, the kid sitting next to me? Does he piss his bed, too?

Even though I'm sitting in the piss section, I like school. I enjoy reading about Dick, Jane, and Spot, and *Green Eggs and Ham*, and *The Cat in the Hat*. Learning is fun! Today we're learning about clouds—stratus, cirrus, and my favorite—the pretty, puffy cumulonimbus ones.

And I enjoy phonics!

Gog.

Gog jogs.

Gog jogs with his *dog.*

Gog jogs with his *dog* and *hog.*

Gog jogs with his *dog* and *hog* in the *fog.*

And I'm making friends easily! One of my new friends, Dougie Osserman, even wrote a funny song about me using the melody of the *Beef-A-Roni* TV commercial. It goes like this:

Beef-A-Roni!

It's made from fake baloney!

Beef-A-Roni aint no good,

chop it up for Peter Wood!

Hooray, for Beef-A-Roni!

Dougie likes me!

I don't hang out with Stick-o anymore.

A Word-Retrieval Problem

I idolize Dougie. He sits up front and his hand is always waving in the air like a fluttering sparrow. Mrs. DeCastro is always calling on him because he's quick, clever, and always knows the right answer. Everyone loves Dougie.

In July, on the last day of class, Mrs. DeCastro says, "Douglas Osserman has never missed a single day of school all year!" We all clap as she hands him the *Attendance Award*. Yes, everyone loves Dougie. And maybe we are a little bit jealous.

Yes, I'm enjoying first grade, but this is when I discover I have a *bigggg* problem besides stuttering and wetting my bed...

I'm sitting in the piss section and I raise my hand.

"Yes, Peter?" says Mrs. DeCastro.

"May I o-o-open the, ah, ah...," I stutter.

She waits for me to finish my sentence.

"May I o-o-open the, ah, ah..." She studies me with her eyes and waits patiently as I scramble to find the right word.

"Window?" she finally says. I nod.

I knew I stuttered, like my dad, but I never realized—until now—that I'm a piss-soaked stutterer with a word-retrieval problem.

After first grade no one ever sees Dougie anymore because he was enrolled in Horace Mann, his father's alma mater, a private school across the Hudson River in Riverdale.

But in my senior year, eleven years later, I spot Dougie sitting at the bottom of his long winding driveway. His hair is long and uncombed, he's wearing bellbottoms, and he's strumming a guitar. Somehow, he doesn't seem to be the same happy Dougie with his hand waving in the air like a fluttering sparrow.

"Hey, Dougie! Remember your *Beef-A-Roni* song?"

He strums a few chords and sings:

> ***Beef-A-Roni!***
>
> ***It's made from fake baloney!***
>
> ***Beef-A-Roni aint no good,***
>
> ***chop it up for Peter Wood!***
>
> ***Hooray, for Beef-A-Roni!***

"So, how ya doin', Doug?"

"Okay," he goes. But he's not *okay.*

That year, his mother found him in their basement dangling from a rope. Unlike my brother's prank, this wasn't a prank. The boy who won the coveted *Attendance Award* in Mrs. DeCastro's first grade class was dead.

You never know how a kid is gonna end up. And that includes me.

Two Warts, Five Allergies, and One Big Fart

The Closter Medical Group is located in town, next to *Wards*. Gram is sitting in the waiting room smoking a Pall Mall while Dr. Nagel is busy cutting off a wart on my middle knuckle and another wart on the web of my left hand. After they're removed, I walk back to Gram all grown-uppy and proud. It's funny how removing two ugly warts makes me feel tough and brave. I wish my word-retrieval problem could be cut out as easily as a wart.

"Gram, why doesn't David get that ugly mole on his chin removed?"

"Ask your mother. To me, it looks like a small chunk of tar on his chin."

"With hairs growing on it."

"It's too bad. He's a very handsome boy otherwise."

*****

I'm always sneezing, wheezing, and rubbing my itchy eyes at home, so my mom brings me to an allergist. While sitting in the waiting room I rip out the **loudest fart in the history of mankind!** It ricochets off the wooden chair and makes it even *louder!*

"Oh, Peter!" gasps my mother.

Cleverly, I point to the man facing us, and blame him. "*You* did it!"

That's when we're whisked into Dr. Picoult's office.

Dr. Picoult is sitting beside a metal tray full of small needles. She goes, "Peter,--just a few *teensy-weensy* pinpricks. Roll up your sleeve."

After 25 *teensy-weensy* pinpricks, she examines the bumps marching up my arm. "Well, Peter—we've discovered why you're sneezing: horses, feathers, dust, dogs, and cats!"

My mother puts her arm around me and whispers, "Don't worry. We won't get rid of Ginger."

The Tonight Show!

Ever since I can remember, my dad's been hunched over his piano trying to compose another catchy melody. And now he has! His song, *The Little Boy,* has hit the Billboard chart and climbing fast!...number 62 last week...this week 32!

The current #1 song is, *I Want to Hold Your Hand* by The Beatles.

Dad isn't all excitey like me, but he's happier than I've seen him in a *looooong* time. The black cloud over his head has lifted and he's even laughing as he watches me do cartwheels on the rug. It's 11:00 and we're patiently waiting for the great Tony Bennett to sing *The Little Boy* on the Tonight Show! I don't know where David is. He's never around much anymore, and that's totally okay with me.

"This is a big b-break," says dad. I know this means a lot to a man who, not long ago, was thinking about jumping off the Brooklyn Bridge. I put my arm around him and squeeze—he hugs me back. I love my dad.

After an *Alka Seltzer* commercial, Johnny Carson goes, "Our next guest needs no introduction..." Tony Bennett emerges from behind a curtain and the band starts playing.

"Dad, I'm so *excited!*"

"Shush!"

As soon as Bennett starts singing, something's not right. His voice is all raspy, the small band lacks the necessary instrumentation, and my dad's beautiful melody is lost...

"I don't even recognize my own s-song," whispers dad. When Bennett finishes singing, he bows, the audience claps, and my dad walks out of the bedroom.

The next week, *The Little Boy* drops from the Billboard chart.

Meet Mr. Schizza

I'm in the third grade now and still wetting the bed and sucking my thumb. *What a baby!*

My mom is now in her early 30s, still young, soft, and elegant. This morning she floats down the staircase and is all smiley and dressy in a floral blouse and a pair of white capris. She sits on our living room sofa. "Boys," she says in her best adult voice, "I have something very important to tell you." She collects her thoughts and goes, "Mr. Schizza has asked me to marry him."

My brother and I exchange glances.

"He's a very nice man and I think he would make a wonderful stepfather." She looks at *the man of the household.* "Do you approve?"

David nods. "Yeah, sure, I guess."

"How about you, Peter?"

My reply is quick. "No."

That's when a car horn honks, followed by footsteps, then a knock at the door. The door opens and in walks Raymond Burr of the *Perry Mason* television show—except it's not Raymond Burr, it's a man who looks like Raymond Burr.

"Meet Mr. Schizza," says my mother.

"Ready?" he smiles. His smile is so loud I can hear it.

"Mr. Schizza is taking us to the circus this afternoon," says my mom.

"Not just *any* circus!" he says, *"The Ringling Brothers Barnum and Bailey Circus—The Greatest Show on Earth!"*

I look at this man, not with fear, but with foreboding. I know I'm looking at my future stepfather.

Six months later, when they marry, me and David move into his large house on Anderson Avenue with his four kids. And it *is* a circus— *The Schizza Circus—The **Worst** Show on Earth.*

My young, soft, elegant mother has gotten me and David trapped in a large house on Anderson Avenue.

Thanks, Mom.

THE SCHIZZA CIRCUS

I hate to witness animals in captivity—or see circus elephants paraded down the streets. When animals are caged, it's a loss of what they are.

K. A. Applegate

Foreign Territory

I'm sitting on the front stoop of Mr. Schizza's house, petting Ginger's furry head. We are both gazing into the woods across the street into Alpine.

Well, Ginger, things are gonna change, I say.

Really? How so? She says, looking up at me.

From now on, you'll be spending your nights outside.

Why?

Because Mr. Schizza doesn't want you inside the house. He doesn't even allow his own dog inside.

Ginger looks at the woods across the street.

But the good thing is you'll be free to explore the forest over there. You'll hunt and climb trees and do whatever you want. And I won't forget to feed you. Your bowl will always be full of food waiting for you at the back door. I pick up Ginger and stroke her fur. *It'll take some adjustment living here but we'll figure it out.*

The front door opens. It's Gram calling me to dinner. "Hurry! Everyone's at the table waiting for you. Leave the cat outside."

You go ahead, Peter, says Ginger. *I'll stay here.*

I kiss her head and walk inside.

At The Dinner Table

All eight of us in this blended family must wait for Mr. Schizza to sit down first. Another rule is everyone must be perfectly polite and demonstrate excellent Emily Post table manners. I would tell you all their names sitting here, but, well, I don't wanna. Besides, they're not important to me, or to this story.

So, we're all sitting here at the table smiling, but I doubt anyone is as happy as they pretend to be. I'm smiling, too, but my hands are twisting a tight knot into my white cloth napkin below the table.

"How's the veal scaloppini?" asks my stepfather.

"Delicious! Yummy!...Wonderful! Tasty! Mouthwatering!" say all my stepbrothers and sisters.

The Schizza house is foreign territory—and David and me are the foreigners. I'm sitting here with two new stepbrothers, two stepsisters, and a stepfather. *(You'd never guess in a million years what would happen to us all: one will try to suicide himself, two will become alcoholic, one will enter a mental hospital, one will escape into the air force, one will become a heroin addict, one will become a successful politician invited to the White House, one will become a successful clothes designer, and one will sell his soul to become a tough guy.)*

After the veal scaloppini, I go outside to play with Ginger but she's not there. I never see her again.

My mother says, "Peter, I think the McBain's dog, next door, got her."

Father's Day at Shea Stadium

Father's Day, Sunday, June 21, 1964

My stepfather loads Rocko, Sally, and me into his big black Bonneville and drives us to Shea Stadium to watch the Mets play the Phillies. Mr. Schizza's cousin is a minor league scout who signed Ed Kranepool, the Mets first baseman. That's probably why we're sitting in loge level seats on the third base side.

But the Mets are losing bad because Jim Bunning, the Phillies' pitcher, has his best stuff—a lively fastball, a darting slider, and a wicked curve. He strikes out Jim Hickman, the leadoff hitter, then batter after batter.

I'm too busy eating hotdogs, Crackerjacks, and drinking Yoohoo and don't really understand what's happening—Bunning is taking a perfect game into the last inning...

Bobby Wine pops out in foul territory...

George Altman whiffs on three pitches...

John Stephenson strikes out on a 2-2 pitch...

A perfect game!

That night Bunning appears on the Ed Sullivan Show, along with golfer Ken Venturi who won the U. S. Open today.

Even though this perfect game will get Bunning inducted into the Baseball Hall of Fame, I was just too busy eating hotdogs, Crackerjacks, and drinking Yooho. The bestest thing about the game was knowing my *real* father was picking me up next weekend to see *Oliver!* — that's a Broadway musical.

(I don't mean to be ungrateful, Mr.Schizza, but there's a big difference between you and my real father on Father's Day.)

41

Palisades Amusement Park

Every night my small transistor radio is tucked between my ear and my pillow. I'm always hoping to hear my dad's song, but I never do. But one song keeps popping up—*Palisades Park*, by Freddy Cannon. It's written by Chuck Barris who later created the *Gong Show* on TV.

"Last night I took a walk after dark

A swingin' place called Palisades Park

To have some fun and see what I could see

That's where the girls are."

This Saturday, Mr. Schizza brings the entire family to Palisades Amusement Park because he's still on the honeymoon period, trying to impress my mom how swell a guy he is. So we all pile into his big Bonneville, with vanity plates, and head to Fort Lee.

"Palisades has the rides, Palisades has the fun—come on over!

Shows and dancing are free, so's the parking, so gee,

Come on over!"

There's a carousel, the fun house, a rickety wooden roller coaster called The Cyclone, the Wild Mouse, a ferris wheel, and *the world's largest salt-water swimming pool.*

But the bestest is the freak show!

Sally, Rocko, and I pay 50 cents apiece to enter a squat concrete building with the dingiest of windows and the muddiest of floors. Sally holds her nose and goes, "It stinks in here!"

Rocko gags.

Inside are glass jars stuffed with deformed animals—two unborn pigs attached at the chest…a three-eyed pig…a cyclops pig…a cat with two heads…two cats with one head…a snake with two heads…

But the stink isn't from the jars—it's from a two-headed cow tied up in back. His right head looks normal-ish, but the left head looks sick with droopy red eyes, its tongue is hanging out, and a thick string of snot is hanging from one nostril.

Suddenly, a long pink tongue from the *healthy-ish* head reaches over and slurps the snot from the sick cow's nostril—licks it clean!

"Gross!" gasps Sally.

That's all we talk about on the ride back home—that long pink tongue slurping up yellow snot. It was well worth 50 cents.

A Boxing Match

Our neighbor, Mr. Snyder, is a former pro boxer. He's holding two sets of Everlast gloves and says, "Boys, c'mon, let's have some fun!"

Me and Rocko stare at Mr. Snyder's flat nose—he calls it his *trophy nose.*

You can always hear Mr. Snyder breathing through his trophy nose, especially when he tells us his boxing stories—like when he stepped on Beau Jack's foot in the gym. *"Here I'm a big heavyweight and I go stepping on the little bastard's toe—I was lucky he didn't clobber me—he was the lightweight champion of the world, for crissake!"*

And there's his motorcycle stories, like when he was a teenager and crashed into a tree. *"Ever since then, I got no sense of smell or taste— everything's sawdust. But, hey, I'm luckier than Chester—he fell off his Harley speeding down a hill—his boot got caught and kept dragging him down. His face was scraped off—teeth, nose, eyes— pieces of Chester everywhere."*

Mr. Snyder holds out the boxing gloves. "Stop stallin'! Lace 'em up!"

"No h-headgear?" I ask.

"Nah, won't need none."

"There's no boxing ring," says Rocko.

"Lawn here's fine," he says.

Rocko is two years older and two inches bigger.

DING!

"Now, don't go haywire, boys," says Mr. Snyder. I'm quickly discovering a boxing match draws a crowd because Sally, Margie, and Clara, our cute neighbor, are sitting on the grass watching. Even Mr. Snyder's German shepherd, locked in the garage, is all excitey banging himself against the door.

"Ding!" calls Mr. Snyder.

Rocko and I cautiously circle each other. I throw a left jab and it lands squarely on his nose.

"Time!" calls Mr. Snyder. Rocko's nose is all red. "You okay?" asks Mr. Snyder.

Rocko nods, but his eyes are watering.

Mr. Snyder steps back. *"Box!"*

I'm discovering boxing is great fun! I'm feeling pretty good dancing around, bobbing and weaving, until Rocko lands a solid shot on the side of my head.

"Time!" calls Mr. Snyder. "You okay, Peter?"

I nod and blink away tears.

He smiles and goes, "Okay, boys, let's call it quits for today." While unlacing our gloves, he adds, "That's what I like, one fighter lands a good shot, and then the other guy lands an even *better* shot!"

Nah, boxing's not so much fun after all, and it bugs me that Rocko got in the last lick. But I remind myself he's two years older and two inches bigger. I don't like it much him landing the last shot. At least there was no blood...but the blood will be flowing later, when Mr. Snyder opens the garage door and his German Shepherd escapes...

A Mauling

…when Mr. Snyder lifts his garage door, out races his German Shepherd…Sally runs home and tells us what happened: "The dog jumped on top of Clara and started biting her face. She was screaming and blood was all over her face and shirt. Mr. Snyder was pulling the dog's tail but couldn't stop him!"

Clara didn't return to school that week, or the following week. When she did return, there was a huge white bandage covering the left side of her face. A month later, when the bandage was removed, red scars were lining her left cheek, running up to her eye.

Five decades have passed and I'm now looking at Clara's face in my 1967 Village School eighth grade yearbook before the attack. What a pretty face.

I decide to call Clara because I want to include this incident for this book—but I want her permission. Would she still be traumatized by a dog who chewed up her face? Should I just skip this chapter?

I finally locate her on line because she's still using her maiden name.

"Hello, Clara?"

"Who's this?"

"Peter Wood."

A long pause.

"I'm your former neighbor from Closter who lived on Anderson Avenue."

"…Oh, yes," she says. "Hi."

With her consent, we discuss the dog attack.

She says, "I've gotten over that day a long time ago. I think it was more upsetting for my parents than for me." I'm searching her voice for emotion and wonder if she's being honest.

"I love dogs," she continues. "I even have one myself. Yes, I might have been scarred physically—but not emotionally." I want to believe her more than anything, but I don't think I do.

"Do you mind if I write about the attack in my book?"

Another long pause. "I'll think about it and get back to you," she says. "I have your number."

She never got back with me.

My Stepbrother and Me

Me and Rocko share a bedroom, but that's all we share. We're brothers without *really* being brothers, and we're friendly without *really* being friends. But I prefer it that way. I want to keep my relationship with him limited, thank you very much.

I don't hate Rocko, I just don't care for his company. How can you hate a kid who lost his mother at the tender age of six? She was only in her early thirties when she died.

My mom tells me Rocko's mother was a devout Christian Scientist, a woman of strong religious conviction who refused medical treatment to fight against the lousy cancer growing inside her belly. Instead of medical attention, she relied upon the Divine Word rooted in the Bible. She trusted her faith in God was strong enough to grant healing. Unfortunately, it didn't turn out that way.

One morning, after years of suffering, Rocko's mother passed away. She was discovered in her parent's Florida home lying dead on a blood-soaked rug.

It must be tough growing up without a mother. Honestly, I'm feeling sad for all the Schizza kids, but that doesn't mean I want to be friends with them.

Losing a parent is the worst. It can really screw you up. Hearing my father say he wanted to jump off the Brooklyn Bridge was heartbreaking enough.

Peaceful Coexistence

Living here with the Schizzas isn't *all* bad. I never go hungry. Mr. Schizza is a very smart attorney who makes tons of money and doesn't mind spending it—especially when he shops at his favorite Italian deli in Lodi.

Compared to dad's constant penny-pinching, the Schizza house is living large. Maybe living here will even educate me somehow.

For instance, I am learning peaceful coexistence. It's probably the same peaceful coexistence Professor Deutsch teaches at Columbia University from books. Me, I'm learning it first hand.

It's *easy*. All you gotta do is don't say what you really think. Just gulp everything down.

I'm here but not *really* here. *Does that make sense?* I avoid getting involved with anyone, and I don't share personal feelings or confront anyone. I ask no questions. I just paste a fake smile on my face and am permanently pleasant. That's what David is doing, too. But his smile is more of a shit-eating grin.

Things are not working out in my head. I hate it here. I *really really* hate it here. I don't wanna be contaminated by this foreign family.

I don't know what David's thoughts are about being trapped here with the Schizzas. He doesn't really talk to me much. I'm just his little brother—just a little shit.

I'm aware this chapter isn't doing me any favors. But that's okay— it's the truth.

The Schizza House

The Schizza house is a five-bedroom ranch, much bigger than my father's Dutch cottage. The façade of their house features white wood on top and a snot-finish brickwork on bottom.

"Snot-finish," Rocko tells me, "means the extra mortar squished between the bricks is left to harden, like snot."

"No, dummy!" clarifies Vinny, his older brother. "It's called *weeping joints*, not snot finish."

The secluded setting of the Schizza house is a perfect location for an Alfred Hitchcock horror film. An escaped maniac from Bergen Pines Mental Institution could easily climb up the weeping joints into my bedroom window and stab me to death. Except this isn't a horror film, it's my life.

But, yeah, their Italian food is delicious: mortadella... gnocchi... focaccia... chicken scarpariello... fusilli... tortellini... tiramisu... spumoni... cannolis.

On other nights, it's prosciutto... crostini... braciola... strozzapreti...veal scaloppini... zeppoles... tartufo, or my favorite— marzipan cookies. All are delish—except for the calamari, which is squid or octopus, I forget which.

At my dad's house dinner is *Hamburger Helper*, instant mashed potatoes, frozen peas, and *Fig Newtons* while listening to Debussy, Nat King Cole, and Ella Fitzgerald on the record player.

Last weekend we ate *Swanson's Turkey TV Dinner,* a leftover can of *Dinty Moore*, and *Chips Ahoy Chocolate Chip Cookies.* Louis Armstrong, The Mills Brothers, and *Trois Gymnopedie* played in the background.

"Where's David?" Dad always asks.

"Dunno." David doesn't spend much time at Dad's house. That's *okayyyy* with me.

Back at the Schizzas, on special weekends, we visit Schizza's parents in Lodi. On the dinner table is always a six-course meal: homemade soup, an appetizer, a salad, two meat dishes, a pasta dish with homemade meatballs and spaghetti sauce, and then a some tasty Italian dessert with coffee. *Living large.*

After dinner, we play *Scattergories*, a brain-game that challenges our thinking skills, or a memory game called *I'm Going on a Picnic and Bringing*. I can't lie—both are alotta fun.

One evening, while driving back from Lodi, Mr. Schizza goes, "Rocko and Peter, would you boys like to attend an amateur boxing show next weekend?"

"Sure!" says Rocko.

"S-sure," I stutter with a half-smile. I've never been to a boxing match before.

AMATEUR BOXING TONIGHT!

7:30

AT LODI HIGH SCHOOL GYMNASIUM

Two kids are up in the ring punching the shit out of each other. We're sitting ringside and I see every punch, hear every grunt, feel every bloody nose, and wince with every knockdown. It's an insane war zone.

Why are these kids fighting each other? Are they enjoying it?

But *something* about this insanity grips me—I don't know what that *something* is, but I'm spellbound.

It's wild, bloody, sick, and totally *fascinating*. Each punch seems to be an explosion of power, a cry of relief, and completely *beautiful*. The exhilaration of seeing a brave kid score a knockout is like seeing him hit a homerun on his opponent's head. Each fight is two angry boys screaming at each other with their fists—*without stuttering!*

Let's face it, boxing is an anti-social sport, and every kid up there contains a certain measure of madness—but they're bravely punching out their madness, sadness, fear, and anger. *I didn't realize any of this stuff then, but I do now.*

At the end of the night, the announcer calls up *The Best Fighter of the Night*. A handsome kid steps through the ropes and a pretty girl hands him a big golden trophy, kisses him on his cheek, and the crowd cheers!

Dang! That's **exactly** what I want for *my* life—a golden trophy, a pretty girl kissing me, and a crowd cheering for *me*!

Now all I need is to be brave enough to step into a ring.

Driving Home from the Fights

I'm being very judgy here, but Schizza's big black Bonneville with leather seats and vanity plates is much better than my dad's Plymouth Valiant.

While driving home, Schizza looks over at us and says "I hope you enjoyed the bouts."

Rocko goes, "Dad, you ever box?"

"I was an excellent student. I hit books instead of people."

"You never hit *anyone*?"

"Well, during World War 2, in China, when I was in the Officer's Intelligence Corp, I hit someone."

"Really?"

"The other officers and I were eating *wanchan*, that's *dinner* in Chinese, and this chink waiter starts petting the hair on my arm like I was a monkey. So I punched him down a flight of stairs."

"Wow!" says Rocko.

"Well, it was wartime. I'm not proud of that now." Mr. Schizza is now looking at me from the rear-view mirror. "Peter, did you enjoy tonight's bouts?"

"Well, Dad, it seems to me that boxing's a pretty sad sport."

"Really?"

"I always thought a kid *played* a sport, but those kids weren't playing. They were *fighting*, that's the exact opposite of playing." That conversation didn't actually happen, but it's exactly what I was thinking. I try a smile and stutter, "Yeah, Dad, it was g-good." It isn't a totally honest answer.

Tonight, lying in bed, which is my favorite thinking place, I'm remembering those boys punching out their hate and anger without stuttering. My eyes are closed but I'm seeing the *Best Fighter of the Night* kid holding his gold trophy and seeing that pretty girl kiss his cheek. I'm hearing the crowd cheering...

I hate fighting. But as I fall asleep, I'm unaware of something quietly seeping deep within me...a boxing virus.

Who Are You Punching?

An Everlast heavy bag and a black leather speedbag are now hanging down in the basement. I'm spend a lot of my time down here—much more than upstairs talking to anybody. Punching a bag feels pretty damn good.

"Who are you punching?"

I turn my head and see my mother sitting on the basement steps. *How long has she been watching me?* I ignore her question, turn my back, and keep punching. I have a real good sweat going and I'm developing my left hook. I don't wanna be interrupted—especially by her.

"Are you angry?" she asks.

I keep punching.

"Are you hitting anyone in particular?"

She's such a jerk. I keep punishing the bag—harder and faster.

"I'm really curious—who are you hitting?"

Why doesn't she just shut the fuck up and leave me alone? I blow snot out one nostril like I saw one of the boys do at Lodi High School.

"Peter, are you hitting *me*?" she asks.

I turn in anger. "Mom! Leave me alone! I'm just hitting a damn bag!" But the truth is I *am* hitting someone.

Down in the Basement

My basement boxing gym is peaceful and undisturbed. The only *disturbed* thing down here is *me*. I don't really belong down here. But I don't belong upstairs, either.

I'm not even a *boy* down here—I'm a little *mole* burrowing into dark soil—my peaceful getaway.

Thanks to my mother, me and David have been trapped in this damn house for five years, and boxing has slowly crawled inside me. Punching feels so good. I punch and punch and punch and punch until the sound of my gasping breath is louder than the confused thoughts in my head. Nickel-sized sweat puddles are lying at my feet beneath the heavy bag.

*What's happening to me? Is boxing answering a need I don't even know I have? Am I catching a disease called **punching**. Did I choose this disease because it benefits me in some way? Is punching a heavy bag and speedbag therapeutic? Or harmful?*

I'm 13 years old and I want to be strong and brave, just like that *Best Fighter of the Night* kid in Lodi.

But the horrible truth is this: I'm really a quiet and peaceful boy—just like my father. We both prefer *avoiding* conflict. But that's a secret I'll never admit to myself because I wanna be tough. I *enjoy* fighting as much as I *hate* it, if that makes any sense.

When you look at it, really look at it, I'm alone down here and my confused brain is squeezed shut like a fist. Something is seriously wrong. There's a puzzle deep inside me.

Maybe boxing can un-puzzle me?

The New York City Golden Gloves—Here I Come!

I might be making a *huge* mistake getting tangled up in this boxing bullshit. I'm basically a pretty nice guy who hates fighting. Is learning to throw lefts, rights, and uppercuts taking a wrong turn?

Fuck it—who cares.

Is punching a heavy bag a solution to something that will make my life better or worse? Is fighting against my nature?

Fuck it—who cares.

If I was Jack Dempsey's son, I'd grow up tough. But I'm the son of two gentle artists.

I don't do introspection too well. Yeah, I have so little insight into myself it's disgusting. I haven't yet read Freud, Fromm, Maslow, and *I'm OK You're OK* or *Jonathan Livingston Seagull*—but I'll read all that stuff later.

But for now, hitting a bag is more rewarding than reading a book.

All I know is this: My young mother divorced my old father…She re-married a rich lawyer with a loud court-room voice…He took her from a small Dutch cottage full of anxiety, worry, and stuttering, to a big house with a refrigerator full of delicious Italian food.

Fuck it—who cares.

I'll never admit this, but deep inside I'm a soft marshmallow, just like my dad. I have no business lacing up a pair of boxing gloves in the basement. A boy doesn't need to punch people to be tough—but I haven't read that book yet, either. It's probably sitting somewhere in the self-help section in the Closter Library.

But, like I said, punching feels good. It relaxes me. That's why I'm in the basement hitting someone's face now. No, it's not my mother's face or my stepfather's face—it's my opponent's face when I fight him in Madison Square Garden—when a beautiful girl will hand me a big golden trophy, kiss me on my cheek, and everyone in Madison Square Garden will stand up and cheer me.

And then everything will be okay. I will be strong and brave and tough and I won't stutter anymore.

But right now I am a little blind mole in seventh grade.

Belle

Belle, the Schizza's pet collie, is forbidden inside the house because she sheds too much. That's why she's chained up in the backyard. The poor dog is always patiently waiting for someone to come out to her doghouse and show her some love.

One hot summer afternoon Vinny went out to feed Belle and discovered her dead. Heat stroke. She was a good dog who was loved—but not loved enough.

No one wanted her dead, but all nine of us—Vinny, David, Rita, Rocko, Sally, me, Gram, my mother, and stepfather—simply forgot about her. We are not bad people, but I think each of us is a big asshole, wrapped up in our own personal problems.

It's too horrible to think about—Belle's tongue hanging out, panting in the hot sun, begging for a cup of cold water. But we weren't paying attention to anybody but ourselves.

Now that I think about it, we are all like Belle—our tongues hanging out, waiting for someone to rescue us.

A Heart-To-Heart with My Mother

"Peter, we haven't spoken to each other in two weeks," says my mother.

"*One* week," I fire back.

"Saying *pass the peas* at the dinner table isn't talking—and you didn't even say *please.*"

She's sitting on her king-sized bed, her legs dangling over the side. Nailed to the ceiling is a gold bed-crown which she bought on her honeymoon in Cairo, Egypt. I finally realize something about my mother—she's far happier traveling around the world and working in New York than staying home with us and being a mother.

(My mom, by the way, once told me she was the reincarnation of Cleopatra—I kid you not.)

I'm now sitting in her yellow satin Louis the XLV chair beside her bed, (shipped from Aix-en-Provence, on another one of their vacations.) I'm staring at her bedroom wall, still sweating from hitting the bags in the basement. I sneak a peek at her face—she's looking at me like a concerned mother looks at a colicky infant. She says, "You spend too much time in the basement." She waits for my reply and gets none.

"Peter, aren't you happy living here with us?" Again, she gets no reply.

"Are you angry with me?"

My stepfather steps into the room wearing a crisp white shirt open at the collar, black slacks, and tasseled shoes. He reaches to the top of his dresser. "Sorry for interrupting—forgot my cufflinks."

"Peter and I are just having a little heart-to-heart." But it's not a *heart-to-heart.* It's not even a conversation. It's more of a *nonversation.*

He heads out, and says, "They're nominating me for the Republican Party State Representative, so I might be home late." He closes the door softly.

"...Are you angry with him?" asks my mother.

I wipe the sweat from my forehead. "Mom, I'm not wasting my fucking time being angry with you or him. When you divorced my father, I divorced you. You are already *erased.*" I don't actually say that, because, I don't even know that's what I'm thinking. It's so funny how little self-awareness a twelve-year-old kid has. So I say nothing.

She begins tearing up. "Peter, don't you love me?" Her words hang in the air. Then she reaches out and places her hand on mine. I pull away.

Tears are streaming down her cheeks and she keeps asking if I love her. The more she cries the more I enjoy it. She reaches out again and I pull away again. Pretty women make shitty mothers.

"Look at me, Peter, please *look* at me!" My mom's a very sensitive woman, a big crier who weeps at anything—movies, *Lassie*, and card tricks. I'm taking great pleasure in hurting her. The more she cries the more I love it. I'm making her heartsick. I cross my arms and feel so powerful. I'm a real bastard.

The tears I *might* feel deep inside myself remain there.

"Don't you love me, Peter?"

"No, Mom, I *hate* you. There's a big fucking hole where my love for you should be. The only parent I love is my dad—the man whose heart you ripped out." I don't say that either because, well, even though it's true, it would be too cruel.

After another long silence, after she composes herself, she says, "Peter, would you be happier if you lived with your father?"

My eyes widen.

I Love My Father, But...

...Peter, would you be happier if you lived with your father?

Well, reader, let me tell you the truth—I've learned to coexist here with all the Schizza gunk—*gunk* is Gram's word. Yesterday, for example. David, who is now 17, stole our mother's purple Firebird and slammed it into the garage. Boy, was Schizza *pissed!* And earlier this month, Vinny tried to suicide himself—*(I'll talk about that gunk later.)*...And Schizza is always throwing Rocko into the bedroom closet each time Rocko fails another class...and Rita, my oldest step-sister is always sobbing on the kitchen telephone each time her boyfriend dumps her...and David got a tattoo on his arm...and Gram is drinking like a fish. But my mother is doing real well in her designing career.

...Peter, would you be happier if you lived with your father?

Well, the problem is this—my father has remarried, and I now have a stepmother and a half-sister. Both are very nice but now I feel like I'd be stepping into a *whole new stepfamily.*

...Peter, would you be happier if you lived with your father?

At dad's house, I'd be coexisting there, too, and I'd miss all the Schizza gunk...the circus...the two-headed cow...Jim Bunning's perfect game...the kid winning a golden trophy...the veal scaloppini, fusilli, prosciutto...Toblerone candy and marzipan cookies...Scatagories...

Where do I go? ... Where do I belong?

The Schizza house is out of control in a *controlled* way, but I've adjusted to it.

...Peter, would you be happier if you lived with your father?

Ravioli…lasagna…cannolis, and gelato are better than worry, anxiety, and having to adjust to a new step-family at dad's tiny cottage on 445 Closter Dock Road.

So I'm staying here—me and my punching bags in the basement. I've learned to like this Squirrel.

And I'm starting to enjoy fighting—at least that's what I tell myself.

THE MIDDLE SCHOOL YEARS

Sometimes I wish people were born with no mouth.

It would eliminate a lot of problems.

The Peter Wood Fan Club

I'm in middle school now and still living with the Schizzas, but believe it or not, I'm more-or-less happy. I don't know how this happened, but I am happy—enough. I'm getting good grades and I have a boatload of friends. The kids in Village Middle School are my *real* family.

Today, when I pass Mrs. Esch's room in the hallway, the sixth-grade girls start screaming. I think it's because I look a little bit like Paul McCartney of The Beatles—plus, I do have a pretty good personality, if I do say so myself.

Some girls have even started a *Peter Wood Fan Club* and girls are passing me love-letters in the hallways. Sometimes red lipstick is smeared on the envelope. Some girls even try to rip off the fairy loop from the back of my shirt for a souvenir. And there's this one girl who won't stop calling me late at night. I don't know how all this started, but it's *very* nice because it balances out my low self-esteem.

Sometimes I feel like I'm the happiest kid in the whole wide world—until today.

Today, the entire sixth grade class is going on an overnight camping trip to upstate New York. We're piling into two *Peter Pan* buses and everyone's laughing and yelling…

Pete, sit with me! Sit with me!

Let's sit together!

Pete, sit with us in back!

I'm sitting quietly in the middle of the bus while everyone around me is jumping, laughing, and standing on their seats making funny faces. But my armpits are sopping wet. What's happening?… *I'm in the midst of a massive panic attack, even though I don't even know what a panic attack is.*

The bus pulls onto Knickerbocker Road. *Why am I freaking out?* I close my eyes and see yellow-stained pajamas and wet bed sheets— they are *my* pajamas and *my* bedsheets. I see the girls in the *Peter Wood Fan Club* mocking me.

Look! Pete wets his bed!

Pete's pajamas are full of piss!

Euwie! Pete stinks!

(Maybe I shouldn't say it, but the truth is Rocko and Sally also wet their beds.)

A Boy Bomb

Weeks have turned to months and months have turned to years. I'm now 14 years old and have developed a serious problem—I'm fighting a lot. Getting hit on the nose isn't fun but slugging someone else's nose is. Yeah, I'm getting pretty good with my hands. I'm play-fighting in the playground, slap-fighting in the boy's bathroom, and have a few good punch-outs in town. And I never lose.

I'm honing my boxing skills and becoming a boy bomb.

But at home, I'm the sweetest little thing! I never argue or voice a difference of opinion. I just hide behind my phony smile. My *family* in this house, all they see is that fake smile. Yeah, I've adjusted—peacefully coexisting. Why would I ever want to open up to these people? I've perfected a perpetual, perfumed, plastic, politeness. *(I like that sentence.)*

I've noticed Mr. Schizza's honeymoon period is over and he's become a loudmouthed bully. Very often he berates us when he thinks we've stepped out of line. In restaurants, when he's too loud and mouthy, the *maître d'* needs to shut him up. I wish someone would reach into his mouth and yank out his tongue by its roots.

"Hey, Dad, doesn't your tongue ever get a little bit tired?" I wanna say, but never do.

He's recently entered local politics and is very successful—that's because he's a perfect blend of arrogance, intelligence, and charm. At home, whenever I hear his Bonneville pull into the garage my flesh crawls—I think everyone's does.

Mr. Schizza is not a bad man—but I hate that we still must wait for him to sit down first at the dinner table, or when he sucks his teeth, or when he taps his fingers on the dinner table, or when he smokes his *Benson & Hedges* cigarettes or when he talks politics. I wish he would just shut the fuck up. We're his little sparring partners—his doomed debate mates. We are all like the red dot in the middle of his dartboard.

Last night at the dinner table he asked Vinny, "What do you think about America's presence in Vietnam?"

"We shouldn't be there," goes Vinny.

"I'd agree with you, son, but then we'd both be wrong."

In his clever manner, he tears us down when discussing hippies or Nixon or marijuana, and, with his hard stare, he never lets us get too big for our britches. That's why I keep my mouth shut—except to eat the spaghetti on my plate. He's not a *bad* man, but it's verbal combat around here. Tonight, at the dinner table while discussing the topic of human nature, he goes, "Mankind, is, by its very nature, bad."

"No—mankind is good," replied my mother.

Schizza smiled and said, "What a *naïve* notion, so easily contradicted by the facts." My mom just looked down and kept eating. No one can stop his monologues because, well, we *can't*. Yeah, he's very clever with his mouth.

"How about you, Peter? Is mankind good or bad?"

"Bad," I say. I continue smiling and quietly twist the napkin in my lap, just like the first day I got here. How am I gonna go toe-to-toe with a skilled lawyer—especially if I suffer from a word-retrieval problem? *How can a little coward like me ever find the courage to stand up to him and be a tough guy?*

But, honestly, I admire him and wish I could talk like him. And I gotta admit, he was nice enough to buy me a set of Everlast boxing gloves and the heavybag.

But he's a bully and I *hate* bullies. My strict motto has always been **never start a fight.** And I never do...*except for tomorrow.*

Is mankind good or bad? I gotta ask my real dad.

Hiding Behind a Tree

I'm hiding behind an elm tree after school, just waiting for Mitch Chapman to walk past me on High Street—then I'll punch his face…I see him now, walking towards me—he's wearing chinos and a new madras shirt. And he's smiling—the bastard is always smiling.

"Hi, Pete!" he goes.

I start whaling away good. *Why am I doing this? Mitch and I are friends. What's wrong with me?* That's when a cop pulls up and throws us inside his squad car—Mitch in back, me in front. The cop looks at Mitch and goes, "Why you starting fights, son?"

Mitch's eyes widen. "Me?"

"A bystander reported two boys fighting, and the boy wearing a madras shirt was the instigator."

"I didn't start it!" Mitch explodes. The cop frowns. "Not according to my eyewitness."

"He *did* start it," I lie. I'm *also* wearing a madras shirt, but mine is faded.

"I'm warning you, son—don't start anymore street fights. Next time I won't be so easy." As Mitch steps out of the cop car I notice he isn't smiling. He's crying.

That night, down in the basement, I'm punishing my heavy bag real good. I'm thinking about me hiding behind a tree waiting to punch Mitch. I'm also thinking about me hiding behind a phony smile for so many years. I realize I can punch the smile off Mitch's face, but I can't punch it off my own.

If I were a psychiatrist, I'd have a field day with myself.

69

Donna's House

"We're going to Donna's after school," says Crow. He winks and I know exactly what he means.

Crow and I are seventh graders and Donna's in eighth. She has the biggest tits in school and likes showing them off with tight shirts and sweaters.

Donna's house is a mile from school. We walk through town, turn left at Gino's Barber Shop, and go down Herbert Avenue till we reach her house close to the train tracks. There are three of us—Crow, Squirrel, (my two sparring partners), and me. We're all buddies and becoming excellent candidates for juvenile delinquency—stealing, fighting, and writing graffiti.

Donna opens the front door. Her big nipples are popping though her tight red shirt. I love that! "Come in. No one's home."

I've never been inside her house. It's nice enough, a split-level ranch with three bedrooms. After talking a little bit about school, she instructs each of us to go into different bedrooms and wait. "I'll come in and see you individually," she smiles.

I walk up a short flight of stairs, enter the bedroom on the left, and wait. A queen-sized bed with a lavender bedcover is along the wall, next to a wooden bureau. A large mirror with neckties hanging off it, is off to the side, so I'm guessing it's her parents' bedroom. After a while, I get thinking—what's gonna happen when she comes in?

I hear Donna giggling across the hall and wonder if she is doing sex with Crow or with Squirrel. While waiting, I start thinking about my brother's *Playboy*—the pretty Arab women with hairy vaginas lying on colorful rugs. Donna is kinda pretty, too. Is she going to be naked when she walks in? Will she lie down on the lavender bedspread and let me touch her tits? Will she ask me to pull down my pants? I hope not.

When she finally walks in, she's fully clothed. "Hi," she says.

"H-Hi."

She walks up close and wraps her arms around my waist and starts kissing my lips. Well, I don't know exactly what to do, so I kiss her back. After a while, I open one eye and she's staring at me. *Dang!*...I finally figure it out—she wants me to slip my hand down under her panties. So that's what I do. This is where it gets weird...I reach down to touch her pussy but all I touch is hair. There's a lot of hair down there—there's hair where her pussy should be. I'm feeling all around searching for a slit or hole, or crack, but I can't find one. I go left and right and then up and down, but there's no hole. She's giggling as my fingers explore her—left and right and up and down. When I reach further down with my middle finger I touch something soft, warm, and gooey, but I don't dare go any further because I'm getting dangerously close to her asshole. Maybe that *was* her asshole, and I definitely don't wanna touch her asshole again.

Donna must've gotten fed up with me fumbling around because she calls Crow and Squirrel into the bedroom and says, "Crow, pull down your pants."

Crow kneels on the lavender bedcover, unzips his fly, and pulls out his cock. It's a massive *monster* cock.

"Holy shit!" gasps Squirrel.

"That's some *meat-gun!*" grins Donna.

Crow's cock is massive—definitely bigger than my little thing and I feel like Tiny Tim.

"Suck it," says Crow.

Donna bends down to get a closer look, then lays his meat-gun in the palm of her hand like she's weighing a salami. She then sticks his meat-gun into her mouth. Knowing Crow's filthy hygiene habits, I'm sure his cock stinks. Sure enough, after a few seconds, Donna starts gagging and runs out of the room.

"Come back here!" hollers Squirrel. He probably thinks his cock was gonna be sucked next. But Donna's already washing out her mouth, guzzling milk from a carton she found sitting on the kitchen counter. When she finishes drinking and puts the carton down, I search her eyes for a look of shame of humiliation. None. She just looks sick to her stomach.

When I leave her house, I walk home sticking out my sticky middle finger so it doesn't contaminate my other fingers. While walking down Closter Dock Road, I'm feeling sorry for Donna. What would her parents think if they knew their daughter invited boys over to do sex? What would they think if they knew she let a boy stick a penis into her mouth? Is she a nympho who just can't help herself? Does she do sex with other boys?

When I get home, I wash my contaminated finger with soap and hot water.

It's all pretty depressing.

St. Mary's Saturday Night Dance

At our eighth grade school dance there's always a *best dancer*—and Crow is always it. He's on his fifth straight dance and his dirty-blond hair's all sweaty. A circle of kids is now admiring his movin' & groovin' to Wilson Pickett's *Land of a 1000 Dances.*

One, two, three

One, two, three

Ow! Uh! Alright! Uh!

Got to know how to Pony

Like Bony Moronie…

We're all *oohing* and *ahhing* each time Crow does one of his famous splits. Each time he drops, I'm imagining his smelly meat-gun slamming onto the floor. I guess it doesn't hurt because he keeps doing it.

Mash Potato

Do The Alligator

Put your hand on your hips, yeah

Let your backbone slip

Do the Watusi…

Suddenly, Paul DeKovessey who always pretended to be Micky Mantle when we played wiffle ball in my father's front yard, cups his hands and shouts in my ear, "Jimmy Quinn's fighting in the parking lot! C'mon!"

In some strange way, this is a life-defining moment because I suddenly freeze—just like my panic-attack in sixth grade on the *Peter*

Pan bus. *Two Peters* begin colliding in my head: Do I stay here with the girls at the dance or go outside with the guys to watch a fight in the parking lot?

Am I a ladies' man...or a tough guy?

A Fight in the Parking Lot

"Get outta here, bitch-boy!" shouts Jimmy Quinn, a tough junior who gets into his fair share of street fights. He's three years older than me and I wouldn't wanna tangle with him.

"*You* get outta here, asshole!" yells a kid with a pointy jaw wearing a muscle shirt. He has that young felon look, an angry sneering face that *needs* to be punched—and Quinn will do it in a heartbeat.

Quinn goes, "I don't like your fuckin' attitude, buddy-boy!"

The crowd is all like, "Knuckle his head, Quinn!"

"He aint knucklin' *nobody's* head!"

Quinn grins. "Don't take this the wrong way, asshole, but you're a fuckin' idiot."

"Oh, yeah?"

"Yeah!"

There's more pushing and shouting and a lot of *You asshole!* And *Your mama sucks!* But after two minutes, they growl themselves out and shake hands. The only fight is inside my head. *Who am I?...a ladies' man or a tough guy?*

Trust Yourself

I'm peopled out.

In a confused chaotic muddle, I walk down High Street. I'm not hating the world or thinking about suiciding myself, but it crosses my mind. My mind is dark as the midnight sky, and I *know* I'm not okay.

I stop in at the Closter Rec, pay the bartender $1.50 and walk down to the empty poolhall in the basement where I'll be alone. There's safety in being alone. I turn on the light.

Get outta here, bitch-boy! Says the pool table.

I choose a stick from the rack but it's crooked, so I put it back.

I don't like your attitude, buddy-boy, sneers the table.

I pick another cue and roll it on the table. It wobbles, so I put it back.

So, you're back here again, huh? Sneers the table.

I shrug.

You're escaping. You're hiding. You know that, don't you? What are you escaping from?

"Not sure."

Don't take this the wrong way, asshole, but you're a fuckin' idiot."

"I am," I nod.

Well, cupcake, you're just like a lot of other frightened eighth graders.

"Except I'm the school president and the most popular kid in town. Kids would love to trade places with me."

So why are you down here?

"Sometimes I hate myself."

Anybody worth his salt hates himself at least five times a day.

"I don't know who I am."

You're only 14. You're not supposed to know who you are. If you knew who you were you'd be a pretty shallow person.

"Everyone loves me except me."

Let me tell you something—There was once a confused and scared little boy, just like you—and he did exactly what you're doing now.

"What?"

Escape. He hid in dark subway tunnels in Brooklyn. But when he straightened himself out he became the heavyweight champion of the world.

"Who?"

Floyd Patterson. Look—you're entering high school in two months. You'll figure yourself out. Have faith. Trust yourself.

"Am I good or bad by nature?' There is no answer, so I keep shooting pool with a crooked pool stick. Talking to a goddamn pool table— something is *definitely* wrong with me.

...Dang! Floyd Patterson!

Summer in Lavallette, New Jersey

Summer is pinball machines and batting cages...running barefoot in the sand and getting splinters on the Lavallette boardwalk...

...Summer is Seaside Heights Amusement Park... the smell of *Coppertone* coconut suntan lotion and pretty girls wearing skimpy bikinis...

...it's sparklers, firecrackers, cherry bombs, and ashcans on The Fourth of July...

...it's Gram shouting, *Wake up and fly right!* As me and Rocko ignore her and run behind the mosquito-fumigation truck—inhaling thick white clouds of *DDT*...

...it's listening to Vinny Sorbello's groovy 45-record collection...discovering *Sh-Boom, Sh-Boom* by the Cords...*Johnny B. Goode* by Chuck Berry...*Alley Oop* by The Hollywood Argyles, *Yakety Yak* by The Coasters, *Mack The Knife* by Bobby Darin, *Get a Job* by The Silhouttes, *Shout* by The Isley Brothers...

...it's reading *The Jack Dempsey Story* from a book-mobile, and devouring every single word while lying under the shade of the boardwalk...

...it's a stranger challenging me to a boxing match and then quickly throwing off his gloves after I land a sweet left hook to his jaw...

...it's a beautiful girl walking along the water's edge with her black pubic hair sticking out from her white bikini...

...it's wicked boners and wet dreams at night in my top bunk...

...it's inviting my *meat-gun* sparring partner, Crow, to spend a weekend...

...it's Crow and me standing at the top of the Barnegat Bay Bridge and jumping into the canal...it's me plunging in first, my foot hitting

78

something like a cinderblock or broken glass... it's me hobbling out of the water with a bloody foot...its getting a tetanus shot...

...Summer is sleepwalking...climbing down from my top bunk...walking across the porch, past Gram, my mom, my stepfather...walking across the boardwalk and onto the beach...walking into the Atlantic Ocean with my bare feet. Someone turns me around, and instead of walking back to bed, I open a car door, and crawl inside....

...Summer is punching waves pretending I'm Joe Louis, Rocky Marciano, and Jack Dempsey...

...Summer is preparing for high school. But, honestly, I haven't prepared much. I've read one book—*The Jack Dempsey Story*. After finishing the last page, I closed my eyes and hoped there was a little bit of *jackdempsey* in me—his courage and toughness.

And that's my summer before high school.

The Day Before High School

I'm lying here in bed thinking about the poster I saw hanging up in the school hallway during today's ninth grade orientation.

Life is About Creating Yourself.

-- George Bernard Shaw

Some teacher pointed to it and said *High school is where you will start to discover who you are.* Well, for now, I'll just be happy being me, thank you. I happen to have been voted the most popular kid in eighth grade and the middle school President.

Yeah, I'm very high status. But I always have to remind myself of that because, deep down, I'm the most *unconfident-confident* kid in the universe. I'm confused and all tangled up. My amazingness has always been diluted by self-doubt. *Why can't I like myself as much as my classmates do?*

Like I said, I don't really hate myself—but sometimes I do. No one knows beneath it all, I'm just a little lying coward with a phony smile. Too many times I'm smiling instead of arguing or sticking up for myself. But in the street I'll kick your ass in a heartbeat.

I'm, basically, a very confused kid. *(I hope you appreciate my honesty.)*

I'm still spending alota time down in the basement punching bags. Sometimes I ask myself, *Shouldn't I be upstairs studying math?* But I'm not a math person. Let's face it, math sucks.

If Emily spent $42 for shoes, and this amount is $14

less than twice what she spent for a blouse, then how

much was the blouse?

Give me a break!

I saw this graffiti written in the school bathroom, and one of my other sparring partners, Frankie Regino, had to explain it to me:

7 OUT OF 3

PEOPLE

STRUGGLE

WITH MATH

Dreaming and Boxing

Sometimes, while I'm punching the heavybag in the basement, there's a nasty taste in my mouth. I still secretly suspect I'm taking the wrong road, but I keep that scary thought stuffed down deep. Honestly, I'm getting pretty damn good with my hands. My left hook, in particular. My hook is coming along very nicely, thank you.

Life is About Creating Yourself.

-- George Bernard Shaw

You don't gotta worry about me, Mr. George Bernard Shaw—I'll create myself, thank you. Just give me some time. I have four years here at Northern Valley Regional High School to do it.

Starting tomorrow I'll be entering high school and I have my wardrobe all planned—a short-sleeve, olive-green banlon shirt from Korvettes, faded Wranglers, and my white high-top Converse sneakers, (which are ripped on the sides from playing basketball at Memorial Field.) And I got a haircut today at Gino's.

I'm itching to see who'll be in my classes and who my teachers are. I can't wait to see what's gonna happen tomorrow, and all the tomorrows after that.

Yeah, eighth grade was *super great*—when it wasn't *horribly horrible*. I'm discovering happiness doesn't come when you want it—it comes when it comes. In other words, happiness comes and goes. I hope high school will have more *super great* days than *horribly horrible* days.

So, I'll start off tomorrow where I ended off—the most adorable and popular kid in eighth grade. Like I said, I'm very high status. I'm not gonna have any problems tomorrow.

During orientation, I also noticed a second poster hanging up in the cafeteria by a drinking fountain...

Never mind searching for who you are.

Search for the person you aspire to be.

-- Robert Brault

Last night I had a strange dream… *Jack Dempsey was sitting at my father's piano playing* **The Little Boy***. There was a cat sitting on his head, my father was doing somersaults on the carpet, and a beautiful girl was walking along the water's edge with black pubic hair sticking out from her white bikini.*

Dreaming and boxing, I think, are two places you can go safely insane and get away with it.

"Dad, is mankind good or bad?"

It's the last weekend before high school and me and dad are playing miniature golf in Closter. We're at my favorite hole where you gotta hit your ball past the spinning arms of a windmill and into a clown's nose. Dad has the orange ball and I chose the green one.

"Green goes first," dad says.

I place my ball down, ready to hit it, but then stand up and say, "Dad, Mr. Schizza was talking at the dinner table last week and he said *mankind, by its very nature, is bad.*"

He smiles. "Well, my lad, he's not entirely wrong."

"Then my mom said *mankind, by its very nature, is good.*"

"Well, she's not entirely wrong, either."

"What do you think, Dad?"

Slowly, he swings his putter back and forth and says, "I t-think ten percent of any population is cruel, no matter what--and ten percent is merciful, no matter what. Eighty percent of the people in this world can be m-moved in either direction."

In the car driving home, dad goes, "Well, what do you think?"

"I think we had a great time today."

He looks at me. "No, I mean is mankind, good or bad?"

"Dad, I think, by *your* very nature, *you're* very good."

He pats my knee and goes, "Like father, like son. You're going to do spectacular in school tomorrow."

HIGH SCHOOL YEARS

"High school is not a place, it's a state of mind."

Frankie Zappa

A Reality Slap

Entering high school is so exciting! But when me and my stepsister, Sally, hop out of my mother's purple Firebird, I know something is drastically wrong...*Nothing happens*! The water doesn't part, no spotlights, no red carpet. Kids are just running around, nervous little things, holding books, brown paper lunch bags, and looking down at their new schedules.

Where is my *Peter Wood Fan Club?* I immediately see life is gonna be more grown-uppy here. No girls pulling my fruit loop off my shirt and no more love letters stuffed in my pockets. The adorable, eighth–grade Pete has evaporated over the summer.

I guess when you are voted *Most Popular* and eighth-grade class president, most people think much more of you than they should, and you convince yourself you're a lot better than you are. I feel like jumping off the Brooklyn Bridge because I have lost everything. I have peaked in eighth grade!

I realize this chapter isn't doing me any favors. It's full of dreadful stuff, and I hear Gram going, *Peter! Wake up and fly right!*

 She's absolutely right. Today is gonna get better--I have gym third period, a ham and cheese for lunch which Gram packed for me, and football practice after school. I happen to be a pretty good football player. I really am.

Gram always tells us, "Any day above ground is a good day."

I'm Not an Overachiever

I'm slogging through high school with C's--maybe an occasional B-- but in gym, I'm straight A. That's all I really care about—sports.

I'm not lying when I say I actually *like* school. I'm beginning to feel comfortably uncomfortable and I enjoy learning a lot of interesting tidbits about the world. Like for instance, yesterday Mrs. Simon, my English teacher, said, *Wherever you stand in New York City, there is always a rat 20 feet away...* Mr. Quad, in science, told us, *There is a species of jellyfish that never dies. It's able to revert back into its adolescent state after going through adulthood, a process that looks remarkably like immortality...*And our math teacher, Mr. Pangburn, told us a good one, *If you traveled around the earth seven times between two heartbeats, you'd be moving at the speed of light.* How cool is that? But then Pangburn totally ruined it by explaining the speed of light with a mathmatic formula on the blackboard.

I'm in Pangburn's math class right now--just quietly sitting in the delusion of safety in the back row. *Delusion is a word I learned in Mrs. Simon's English class. It means, maintaining false beliefs even when confronted with facts.*

Why am I even sitting in Pangburn's high-level math class? I don't belong sitting with these stupid brainiacs like Gary Peterson, Nancy Windeknecht, and Gerald Richman who probably live in happy families and enjoy sitting together at the dinner table. (By the way, I realize *stupid brainiacs* makes no sense.)

Right now I'm looking up at the clock while everyone else is hunched over eagerly solving a math problem. I have enough *real* problems to solve, thank you. When I get tired of looking at the clock, I cross my legs and practice writing my name on a piece of graph paper. I have eight ways to write my name, but haven't figured out which is best. I look back up at the clock and cross my legs the other way.

After a week of math-torture, I'm dumped into a lower level. This new math teacher is okay, but there's a problem—big-titted Brenda Heck is sitting in the third row. She's always nibbling and licking the eraser at the end of her pencil, and I'm always getting a wicked boner just watching her.

Dear Reader--I realize this is, yet another, chapter that isn't making me look too good.

Mrs. Simon's English Class

Mrs. Simon is a tough old bird from West Virginia, a down-to-earth teacher with a severe gray hair-bun, but I like when she discusses poetry because she's not all frilly and romantic. And I like her calm way of looking out the window at the bushes and trees when thinking about the best way to explain things to us.

And Mrs. Simon might even *like* me. She says I have "an interesting way of writing."

And I like the books she assigns—*Of Mice and Men, To Kill a Mockingbird,* and *Catcher in the Rye*. Reading books gets me smart because I end up learning groovy new words like *stigma, prattle, pithy, lugubrious, feckless, eclectic, casuistry, noisome, delusion, symbiosis, quisling*. I like the sound of *quisling*.

Unfortunately, the book we're now reading sucks--*The Merchant of Venice*. I find myself reading the same sentence over and over again. I find myself reading the same sentence over and over again. I find myself reading the same sentence over and over again. So I went to the Closter Plaza and picked up *Manchild in the Promised Land* from the Woolworths bookrack. The back cover says it's an urban adventure about *a "Negro from slum Harlem who pulls himself up from the gang wars, the stealing, and the drugs to become a successful law student at one of America's leading universities."* It's 429 pages thick, and I'm very proud of myself for buying such a fat book.

When Mrs. Simon sees me reading *Manchild* instead of *Merchant,* she reads the back cover and says, "I don't think we should use the word *Negro* anymore."

"Why not?"

She looks out the window and then looks back at me. "It's archaic." She notices my confusion and points to the dictionary on her desk. "You're smart. Look it up."

"arkaic… arkcayic…arcaic…" I discover it means "very old or old-fashioned."

Yeah, I'm smart--the smartest *dumb* kid in Mrs. Simon's class.

A Bully

I'm very self-conscious. Everyone stares at me when I walk into the school cafeteria--I know they are, I *smell* it, even though they probably aren't.

But I'm looking at them, too. All these kids are eating tuna fish and P&J sandwiches while pretending they're happy--but I know their smiles and laughs are phony. *All* high school kids are like that. They *pretend* happiness--just like I pretend self-confidence.

Believe it when I say, there's a lot of turmoil and hidden pain beneath our smiles. We're all secretly wrestling with teenagerness—thrashing around with tangled thoughts, think-twists, and fragile egos.

It's hard for me to attend high school and hang around my classmates for too long. We have too many silent grudges, murmuring resentments, penis problems, breast issues, self-esteem dramas, ghetto attitudes, loud anger, and self-mutilation issues. I could go on.

I can barely tolerate my own emotional problems.

But there's one thing I will *never, ever, ever* tolerate--bullying. *(I still feel guilty about punching Mitch.)*

This September, when a greaseball senior was shaking down a scrawny freshman in the cafeteria, I stuttered, "L-Leave him a-alone." I *hate* when I stutter--it makes me look weak.

"Screw you," he goes.

That's all it took. I throw my left hook and we both slide across the lunch table, me on top, punching, punching, punching…

Mr. Colantoni, our tiny hard-ass principal, called Gram into his office and said, *Don't repeat this, but the entire school is very happy what Peter did because this other boy has been a bully ever since he's entered this school, but school rules is rules.*

We were both suspended four days.

When Gram drives me home, she yells, "What's wrong with you? Wake up and fly right!... What kind of sandwich you want—ham and swiss or tunafish?"

Denise Falasca

Denise was a real cutie pie. I say *was* because she was murdered last week. She was hitchhiking and some perv picked her up and strangled her with the *crucifix necklace around her neck.* That's what the newspaper reported. Her body was dumped in Saddle Brook next to a cemetery.

Denise was fifteen.

That's why today's so sad. I'm watching her coffin being lowered into a big dark hole, dirt is being shoveled onto it and she's being swallowed up by darkness. I can't believe cute, little Denise is lying in that box. Her body will now rot and crumble into mildewy pieces.

I still have a crush on Denise. She's still a petite little girl dancing in bare feet on Brenda Heck's blue shag rug. She's still giggling and singing *Mrs. Brown, You've Got a Lovely Daughter.*

Oh, it's so awful to think that Denise's body will eventually turn into a *worm farm—that's a line in one of e.e. cummings' poems.*

*****

Denise's murder went unsolved for five decades until Richard Cottingham confessed. Cottingham has been serving a 200-year life sentence in the New Jersey State Prison for picking up hookers, tying them up, torturing them--some were dismembered and beheaded.

*Denise was **not** a hooker.*

*I spit on the book written about him—**The Torso Killer.***

Death

*Death...*Ginger was probably eaten by a dog, we accidently killed Belle, Denise Falasca was murdered, and last night, Vinny, my oldest stepbrother, tried to suicide himself. Here's what happened: When a girl refused his invitation to the senior prom, he dug into the medicine cabinet and swallowed every last Excedrin. When David found him dying in bed, he called out to my stepfather who then dragged Vinny around the house, pleading, *"Vomit! Vinny, Vomit!"* Vinny's mouth was hanging open and groaning, but he couldn't puke. So an ambulance rushed him to Pascack Valley Hospital to get his stomach pumped.

Vinny is the apple of Mr. Schizza's eye. He was voted "Most Friendly" in his Old Tappan High School yearbook--he's a starting halfback on the football team, he's handsome, and an excellent student--but shit happens

*****

It's Friday night at dad's cottage—a whole different world from The Schizza's house--and I'm still hearing Mr. Schizza plead, *"Vomit, Vinny, Vomit!"* I'm lying on the floor, looking up at my favorite celebrities tacked on my bedroom wall—singer Rita Coolidge...The Kinks...Y.A. Tittle, Spider Lockhart, and Frankie Gifford of the New York Giants...Bat Battalio, an old-timey prizefighter, and Emile Griffith, the Middleweight Champion of the World. Emile begins whispering to me about death... *Peter, death sneaks up on us. Sometimes it comes out of an Excedrin bottle, or it's a flat-out blunder like with Belle, or it's a murdered girlfriend. Sometimes death creeps forward quietly, like Vinny's depression, or his mother's stomach cancer...Sometimes death comes in the boxing ring.*

"You killed Benny "Kid" Paret in Madison Square Garden with landed 28 unanswered punches to his head. I watched it on tv with my dad."

Peter, boxing is a dangerous sport--you sure you wanna sign up for the New York City Golden Gloves?

"Yes."

And risk death?

"Yes."

To become a New York Golden Gloves champion?

"Yes—like you were."

And fight in the very same ring I killed Benny "Kid" Paret?

"Yes."

Beware of what you want, Peter, because you might get it.

Me and Vinny

Me and Vinny, my oldest stepbrother, are similar but different. We are dead at home but alive at school. He was voted "Most Friendly" and I was voted "Most Popular." But at home I'm not *Most Popular* and he isn't *Most Friendly*--at least to me. I don't really give a rat's ass because I don't like him much. I'm sure the feeling is mutual.

And we both have lost our mothers.

Ever since he started calling me a *mama's boy*, I've avoided my mother. That's on *me*. I started shunning her, even hating her. Basically, I threw her away like a piece of garbage, just like she threw away my old failing father. So, neither of us have a mother. Really, I could give a shit.

No one wants to be called a *mama's boy*.

This is another chapter that doesn't make me look good.

The Hirsch Brothers

Bob Hirsch, a tough senior on our football team, is coming over to spar--but I didn't invite the guy with him. "Marty's my brother," says Bob, "he boxes in the army."

Marty is wearing a flesh-colored rubber sweat-suit and a pair of boxing gloves is strung over his shoulders. He aint smiling.

Down in the basement, Marty is already lacing up his gloves--and still hasn't cracked a smile or said hello. He's eight years older than me and it's obvious he's not the friendly type. "Marty, what's your damn problem? Why do you wanna kick my ass?" I wanna say that, but don't.

*****

Bob and I start sparring, just dancing around, pulling punches. After three rounds, Marty pops up. "*My* turn!" He begins shadowboxing and it's obvious--he's a ringer who knows to plant his feet to maximize punching power. The bastard probably has a ton of knockouts.

Sure enough, he starts whacking me silly. I'm jabbing and dancing, but there's no safety with Marty—he's beating me up good. After three rounds of pain, humiliation, and a nice nosebleed, Marty pulls off his gloves with his teeth and smiles, "Thanks, I enjoyed that." *Of course you did, asshole! Beating me up musta been a lot of fun!*

Turns out, Marty is a pretty nice after that--he's just suspicious of anyone who might want to hurt his younger brother.

I wish David cared about me like that.

*****

After they leave, I put an icepack on my nose. Blood's trickling out and I feel my nose shifting left to right. Inside sounds like cracking peanut brittle. *Dang!* I've always wanted a broken nose and now, thanks to Marty, I got one.

The next morning I have two black eyes and I can't close my jaw. I look in the mirror confirming my features with the touch of my hand. Nose? *Here!* Chin? *Here!* Eyes? *Here!* Teeth? *Here!* This insane facial roll-call is…well, *insane.*

*****

Jake LaMotta, the former world middleweight champion once said, "My nose was broken six times, my hands six times, a few fractured ribs, fifty stitches over my eyes. But the only place I got hurt was out of the ring."

*****

Emile Griffith whispers: *Beware of what you want because you might get it.*

"We're Friends, Right?"

I'm walking to the beat of a different drummer. While most sophomores are watching television, joining school clubs, or beginning to think about college, I'm inviting kids over to my house to box. By the way, I learned that line, *"walking to the beat of a different drummer"* from *Walden*, a book we read in Mrs. Simon's English class.

*****

Now I'm at Ralph Bibeau's house after school waiting to slap-box somebody. Ralph's parents aren't home, and if they knew Ralph invited 13 punks to hang out in their carpeted living room, they'd have a shit fit.

I know Ralph only from the school hallways. He's three years older and cocky in a humble sort of way, if that's even possible. He reminds me of David--both are greasers with duck-ass haircuts, both hang out at The Taaz pool hall, both sing acapella at night on street corners, both are handsome and haughty, and both have a bunch of girlfriends.

Right now, eight sexy girls are sitting around the living room. Each is dolled up with tons of makeup. Their hair is teased and I wonder which ones sprinkle sugar in their hair, or iron it on an ironing board. I bet each one does sex.

They're laughing and clapping as us stupid boys try to impress them by slapping each other. I feel a rush of excitement and a pang of fear as I wait my turn. Fear is grabbing me by the stomach, but I do what I always do when that happens—ignore it.

"We're friends, right?" smiles Ralph.

"Yeah," I go.

"Good!" Then he jump-starts our friendship with eight quick slaps. Slaps are coming at me from all angles. *Slap! Slap! Slap!* He's whacking me good. Whatever he's doing is *genius. Slap! Slap! Slap!* He's switching lefty and righty and rocking back and forth--typical street-fighting crap he's probably perfected on in Hackensack or Newark. The girls are laughing as he smacks my face red, and my nose starts bleeding. *Dang!*

The center of my universe, at this very second, is Ralph's carpeted living room--his house on Harvey Street--in Closter--in Bergen County--in New Jersey--and I'm getting whacked in this fucking universe. My face is stinging, my ears are ringing, and blood is dripping down my lip. *This is so damn humiliating!* Eight pretty girls with tons of makeup and teased hair are laughing at *me!*

Ralph, this is a hell of a way to treat your friend!

I'm fighting back but I feel like a lump of human lard—*slow and stupid.* I kid you not—I'm trying my best, but slapping Ralph's face is like drinking soup with a fork.

Afterwards, Ralph is all apologetic and goes, "Hey, that was fun, huh?"

"Kinda," I go.

Ralph is, basically, a good guy. He just kicked my ass in a disciplined and methodical fashion, and he taught me an important lesson. The lesson is this: If I'm gonna fight in Madison square Garden one day, I need to get *tougher, faster,* and *smarter.* I vow to do whatever it takes--even if I have to pull, dig, or squeeze courage out of my penis—I'll do it.

As I walk home, up Ruckman Road, I'm kinda happy because I didn't get any blood on Ralph's parents' carpet.

The Girl with a Horsewhip

My feelings about Brenda Heck are not complicated—I want to put my penis into her vagina. That's a true fact. She's a real sexpot and her body rocks in a big way. She's always prancing around with her proud breasts bouncing up and down. She's a total flirt who knows exactly what she's doing when she nibbles the eraser at the end of her pencil or when she--accidently on purpose--drops something on the floor, bends over, and sticks her butt high in the air for everyone to admire. I'm absolutely *positive* we all secretly masturbate to her in our bedrooms--probably teachers, too.

Right now I'm walking down Knickerbocker Road to her house. It's between football double sessions, and I know Coach Sgro will kill me if I don't get back to practice on time. But I'm hoping I'll get lucky and grab a quick piece of ass before I return to practice.

It's not long before Brenda and I are lying on her sofa petting each other. It's nice and intimate, the worst time to have smelly armpits, egg breath, or crack a rat. I go, "Remember the first time I m-met you?"

"No. Tell me."

"You were chasing Gerry Savianeso around your front yard with a horse w-whip."

She chuckles. "Let's kiss--not talk."

I don't think chasing a boy with a horse whip is healthy human behavior, do you?

"Why were you chasing him?"

"Oh, I don't remember," she says.

As we're smooching, I'm wondering if Brenda has some deep subconscious hatred for men. Maybe she's angry at her father who chose to move Upstate New York to train horses rather than live with his family? I don't know. I'm just a freshman in high school, not a psychiatrist.

She's been sticking her tongue inside my mouth all this time. She's now letting me unbutton her jeans and permitting me to slip my middle finger in and out of her sweet spot. Her eyes are closed, her lower lip is jutting out a bit, and she's moaning. Very quickly, a warm milky-white puddle collects in the palm of my hand. I don't know what it is and I don't wanna know. *Is it sweat? Piss?* I don't want to embarrass her, so I quietly wipe it on her shag rug. But quickly, another white puddle collects in my palm, so I wipe that on the rug, too.

Afterwards, in the kitchen, we're eating sandwiches before I head back to practice.

"*Oh*, that was so much fun," Brenda says, pulling me back to the sofa. "Let's do it again."

"No, I got football." *I remind myself I'm a tough guy not a lady's man.*

Her pretty brown eyes rim with tears and she pouts, "You love football more than me."

"If I'm late, Coach'll have me running sprints till my legs puke."

"You scared of an old stupid coach?" That's when we start bickering. Brenda and me bicker a lot. I'm guessing it's her unresolved daddy issues. Before leaving, I punch a hole in her kitchen wall because, well, because I'm a tough guy, not a lady's man. *I might have some unresolved mommy issues.*

Well, anyway, I'm not too worried about the hole in the wall because her father lives far away with his horses.

She, at least, could've given me a handjob.

Sitting in a Classroom

I'm sitting in Mr. Quad's biology class with sweaty palms, even the bottom of my feet in my ripped high-top Cons are sweaty. I don't look anxious or nervous—but I am. I don't let anyone see what a low self-esteemed mess I am. *What's wrong with me?* Maybe it's not in my nature to be confident. Maybe God forbids it.

Mr. Quad is going, "Mitochondria are concerned with the respiratory...*blah, blah, blah.*"

Dang! I always have difficulty concentrating and I'm so easily sidetracked. Like when a teacher erases the blackboard and misses a tiny part of a word--I wind up staring at that partially-erased word for the rest of the class. I even lose focus when someone's shoe makes a fart noise, or when a speed-reader, like Billy Hall, turns the page before I do, or when Brenda Heck tongues her eraser. I'm so easily distracted it's disgusting. *I have monkey mind.*

That poster in the school hallway lied. It said, *High school will teach you who you are.* Well, it's doing a *better* job teaching me who I'm *not.*

Well, who am I?

The essential question is: *Where do I belong?* Because it's not in the math club...or the art club...or the debate team...or the marching band or in orchestra...or the theatre club...or the National Honor Society, *(that goes without saying!)* But, honestly, I could give a rat's ass--as long as I belong *somewhere.*

My *somewhere* is the playing field. I'm the starting halfback, the starting centerfielder, and I hold my own brawling on the street. So, I guess that's where I belong...*me and sports.*

Two Peaceful and Sensitive Boys

Even though I've been fighting a lot, I suspect everyone knows I'm not *really* tough. I'm still the same little boy who plays the alto saxophone in the school band, looks at my stamp collection *(stamps from Laos, The Congo, and Monaco are the prettiest),* still attends church, and still kisses my dad when I visit him. (I even playfully lick his cheek when we watch TV together because I like how his whiskers scrape my tongue. *Weird, I know.)*

I'm still struggling with this: *How can I grow up to be a tough guy when my peaceful parents are sensitive artists?* Something went wrong along the way because there is *nothing* artistic about me. And I'm fighting in the street.

During my first three years in high school, I've broken a kid's jaw, taken a kid's front tooth out, and severely damaged a senior's right eye—his graduation picture is proof.

I won't go into the details about those fights, which I'd be happy to discuss, but won't because it might sound braggy. But I will say this, wiseass Jack Lazarko deserved his broken jaw—he was from Riverdell High School who was all, *Fuck you! Fuck you!...*And six-foot-one, 220 pound, Kenny Mattern, deserved getting his tooth punched out because he was all, *I could beat you, Wood! You ain't so tough!...*And Todd Brinkerhoff earned his damaged eye because of arrogance and stupidity. He never shoulda elbowed past me and my two sparring partners, Crow and Squirrel, as we walked down Durie Avenue. "Holy shit!" yelled Crow. "You punched him across the road!"

"That Chevy almost slammed into you guys!" laughed Squirrel.

"He learned a lesson--*Don't bark if you can't bite*," I said.

Skipping School

I skip school when I'm feeling sad, scared, or depressed. I *love* skipping school—I'm sick of teachers and coaches controlling my life. Sometimes I just need to be alone. But I also know skipping school is a weakness--that's why I *hate* skipping school.

Skipping school is not what a tough guy, like me, should be doing.

This morning I'm skipping again. I'm walking down Knickerbocker Road and my hands are dug into my pockets because it's cold, but it'll be nice and toasty inside the Rec pool hall when I get there. I know deep inside me there is something good and strong--something that makes me feel happy about myself. Sometimes I feel it, but today is *not* that day.

I'm happy to be walking alone, but it's a shallow happiness because I know I'm being fragile. I try to convince myself I'm no different than any other 15-year-old boy--my body is growing, changing, sprouting hair, my voice is cracking, and I'm always getting wicked hardons-- like *always!* The difference is, I have the guts to play hooky every now and then, and most kids don't. *But that's a lie. I'm being weak.*

It occurs to me I am very confused. What series of mistakes and faults have led me to this low point this morning? I wanna be tough and strong but *I'm not.* Honestly, it's the softness and gentility of my father that I see within me that I respect most. I'm so proud to be my father's son --but I'm also ashamed because a nice sweet nature isn't an asset on a football field or in a street fight. Let's face it--sports and fighting is more masculine than writing a sweet melody. There's a lot of wrongness to my thinking, I'm aware of that.

Yes, I'm very tangled up. I'm a stranger to myself. I don't know Pete, but I am him.

The Closter Rec

Somehow, the Closter Rec has claimed me. It's warm and quiet inside and I kinda envy the old men sitting on the bar stools. They're free to watch *Gunsmoke* and *Gilligan's Island* on the television, play checkers, and drink beer all day if they want. No teachers, coaches, or parents are bugging them.

When the bartender sees me walk in the door so early in the morning his eyebrows raise, but he just hands me a rack of balls and I walk down into the basement.

...Ah! The feckless young man is back again...

I dump the balls on the table and start shooting.

...You don't mind if I say 'feckless', do you?...

I rack up the balls.

*...Peter, you're self-destructive, you realize that, don't you? Life isn't beating you down--**you're beating yourself down**...*

I chalk up my stick. "You don't like me, do you?" I go.

...I don't like what you're becoming...

"What's that—Floyd Patterson hiding in a subway tunnel?"

...No. One of those defeated old men upstairs...

"You think?"

...Peter, let me ask a question--What's your biggest weakness?...

"My biggest weakness is...me. I'm weak."

...Really?...

"And stupid."

*...No, your biggest weakness is you **believe** you're weak and stupid. You're plagued by self-doubt. Your negativity is swallowing you up. You have the "**Fuck Me Disease**."*

"'Wake up and fly right', is what my grandmother says."

...That's because you're ungrateful for everything you have—a loving mother and father, a wise grandmother, a roof over your head, and food in your belly. You're healthy, smart, and popular. Yet you're full of unhappiness...

"So?"

...Your unhappiness is splashing onto everyone—and you've become too dependent on boxing...

"Is that a problem?"

...Boxing is the gutter of sports...

"It's making me a stronger person."

...Can't you conceive of anything healthier to do?...

"Like what?" I suddenly realize I'm sweating and breathing hard. This is *way* too much introspection. *Introspection* is a word Mrs. Simon taught us. It means *looking into yourself.* It's so exhausting being me. "I'm weak and stupid," I whisper.

*...That's your **Fuck Me Disease"** talking." One day you will read "How to Be Your Own Best Friend", "The Art of Loving", "Man's Search for Himself", "The Art of Thinking", and many other great books...*

"I feel like there's a scream in me trying to get out."

...Every artist, writer, painter, dancer and musician has their scream. But they don't need to get punched on the nose or get their brains scrambled. Peter, there's a healthier world outside of boxing

waiting to be discovered. Read books! It's not an accident that a book opens just like a door...

"Mrs. Simon always says that."

...Listen to her—Listen to all your teachers...

"Oh, and by the way, I know what 'feckless' means."

...Because you didn't skip school that day...

Something is Wrong with David

I catch my brother nosing around in our mom's walk-in closet. There's a ton of expensive crap in there—high-heel shoes, designer dresses, jewelry, wigs, and hats. I see him admiring himself in the mirror wearing our mother's purple velour caftan.

"What're you doing?" I ask.

He grins and goes, "Well, I like to drive around in mom's car at night while wearing this."

"Why?"

"It makes me feel like an African tribal chief."

What's wrong with this guy? I know it's quite confusing for people to believe, but I still love him even though we don't have a close relationship. He's always teasing or mocking me and it's been that way since forever. I accept it because I've learned that's what an older brother does.

Recently, he told me, "Sometimes I pop a tab of speed." I wonder if he does that while driving around in that purple caftan thingy. "Don't tell anyone," he said.

I guess I should tell *someone*. But I just kept my mouth shut.

A Meatball in David's Ear

Tonight at the dinner table David went *waaay* too far. Him, Sally, and me are sitting at the table eating spaghetti and meatballs. He's sitting in our stepfather's chair acting like a big hotshot, mocking my stutter. I ignore the bastard until I pick up a meatball from my plate and slam it into his ear. *SPLAT!* Very quickly I'm lying on the floor with the bastard kneeling on top of me, yelling, *I'll kill you! I'll kill you!* His fist is in my face but he doesn't have the guts to punch me.

Seeing the side of his face dripping with Ragu spaghetti sauce, and a meatball wedged in his ear is totally worth it!

I bet he's gonna pop a tab of speed tonight and drive around in that purple caftan pretending he's an African chief.

The Best Punch I Ever Threw

It's been very challenging for me to hold onto a warm sense of brotherly love for a guy who's always been such a dickhead. I'm fed up with David calling me a *mama's boy*...I'm tired of him mocking my stutter...I'm fed up with him blowing smoke-rings in my face...and I'm still angry at him for burying me up to my neck in sand at the Jersey Shore, dropping a tin pail over my head, and then walking away with his friend. He hates me. But at least he hasn't tied me up like he did Ginger.

I love David, but I think I hate him more.

Today, when he stole $10 from my wallet, I had enough. "Wanna box me down in the b-basement?" I stutter.

"S-Sure," he mocks.

We put on the gloves and start moving around. He's bigger, older, has a longer reach, but I think I've figured him out and have the exact move to kick his ass. I've fantasized about this moment: I'll feint a right to his head, step low inside, and without warning, spring up with a left hook to his head.

SPLAT!

After my punch lands flush on his jaw, David throws off his gloves, stomps upstairs, muttering, "Fuck this shit!"

You may think it's impossible for a fifteen-year-old kid to instantly grow ten feet tall, but it happened tonight. It's amazing what happens when you face your fears and throw a good left hook.

No Pain—No Gain

I'm pedaling as fast as I can down in the basement. Sweat's dripping down my cheeks and soaking into my socks. I'm gasping for air.

Go faster, you happy horse-shit! Go faster!

I'm standing in the pedals of an Exercycle, hunching my shoulders over the handlebars, pumping my legs as hard as they can go. *(Since my stepfather got bored with the Exercycle and only used it to hang his shirts and ties on the handlebars in his bedroom, he asked Vinny, Rocko, David, and me to lug it down to the basement, where it is now, near my heavy bag.)*

Is that all you got? barks Coach Sgro.

I'm trying to go faster but my asthma is kicking up. Asthma sucks.

Faster, you happy horse-shit!

"I'm *trying*!" My legs are burning, I'm panting hard, and hot sweat puddles are splashing onto the floor.

*There's no **trying** to it! yells Coach. There's only doing—or not doing! Trying is when you were five years old and got credit for tying your shoelaces! Let's go, you happy horse-shit!*

Coach is *always* with me--yelling, pushing, judging. He's called me a *happy horse-shit* a million times and shouted...*No pain no gain!* another million.

I *am* a horse shit—but not a happy one.

Coach Sgro

Coach Sgro is insane. I once overheard him tell his assistant coach, *Some kids ya gotta beat with a stick, others ya gotta be gentle.* I think I'm the kind he beats with a stick because he's always calling me a *happy horseshit.*

Before Sgro coached at our school, he and Vince Lombardi coached at St. Cecilia's--a fierce football powerhouse. To clarify: Vince Lombardi had coached the Green Bay Packers--another fierce football powerhouse. Both are football tyrants.

One summer, to get a jump on the competition, Sgro secretly organized an illegal football practice outside the state of New Jersey—that's when one of his linemen died of heat exhaustion because Sgro had denied the kid water. The St. Cecilia's football program was banned that year.

Sgro, somehow, was hired at our school and brought the Lombardi's hot temper, verbal abuse, and perfectionism with him. He's always shouting Lombardi-isms...*Winning isn't everything, it's the only thing... Show me a good loser, and I'll show you a loser...Practice doesn't make perfect--only perfect practice makes perfect.* And my favorite--*If you aren't fired with enthusiasm, you will be fired with enthusiasm.*

We all fear Coach Sgro. His heart is a dry bone and *nothing* you do is ever good enough. But everyone respects the bastard.

Football practices are like entering a meat grinder. Afterwards, we're slumped on the locker room floor, bloody, sweaty, and exhausted. That's when we have to listen to his loud shouty pep talks. But, honestly, I get more fatherly advice from him than from my father and stepfather combined...*Football is like life -- it requires perseverance, self-denial, hard work, sacrifice, dedication and respect for authority... People who work together will win--whether it's football, or the problems of modern society...I am preparing you boys for life!*

One day last spring, Coach Sgro walked up to me on the baseball diamond and goes, "Pete, you know what I like about you?"

"W-What?"

"Your mental toughness."

"Coach Sgro, you are a great coach, but you're a *very poor* judge of character," is what I wanted to tell him.

My Dad

There's no blood on my father's white shirt but his hair's all mussed and his right hand is in a plaster cast.

"Broke my thumb, matey."

We're standing next to the goldfish pond, and Dad, always a proper Englishman, is wearing a striped tie with a tie-clip and his clip-on suspenders.

"What happened, Dad?" I'm sure the miniature golf we had planned for today is probably out the window.

"Well, last night, my lyricist, Sammy Gallop and I were working late on a melody. When we left my office it was dark because the hall lights were shut. That's when I spotted someone walking toward us— the panhandler on Broadway who always curses me when I don't give him money. I whispered, *Sammy, hold my valise, mate*. As the bloke walked closer, what was flashing through my mind were you, David, Sarah, and Jane. What would happen if something happened to *me*? As soon as he got closer, I made a fist and punched as hard as I could and his head hit the floor with a bang. *My God!* said Sammy. *You killed him!*

Dad isn't taking pleasure in telling this story--but *I* am. I'm busting with pride! My gentle dad *punched* somebody! I'm in total awe!

"Did you?" I ask.

"Did I what?"

"Kill him?"

"Heavens, no! I nudged his head a wee bit with my shoe. He was still breathing."

How cool is that? My dad knocked someone out! His hands always reminded me of two hairy animals scooting across the piano keys--

not a mallet! *Maybe there's a little bit of jackdempsey hiding inside my dad!*

"Were you scared?" I ask.

"Yes, lad." Dad makes a fist with his left hand and asks, "When you make a fist, does the thumb go inside or outside?"

I laugh and hug him. No, Dad isn't a tough guy. He's a gentleman who wears glasses, clip-on suspenders, stutters, and doesn't punch people. He's a softy who doesn't like confrontation. He doesn't even know how to make a fist! But he will kick your butt if needed. I'm *sooo* proud!

"Well, matey, let's have that game of miniature golf, shall we?"

When I go to bed tonight, I realize Dad told me the whole story without stuttering once. I fall asleep feeling strong.

Crow, Squirrel, and Me

I'm sitting in the driver's seat of my mother's purple Firebird. Tonight, when she went to bed, I snuck out with her car keys. It's three in the morning, everyone's fast asleep, except for me and my two sparring partners--Crow and Squirrel. When I pick them up, they're wearing pajamas, too.

We go cruising down Closter Dock Road, driving up High Street, going by Memorial Field, then doing it all over again. We're exploring our hometown!

"Merrily we roll along, roll along...Merrily we roll along, roll along!" sings Squirrel.

When we drive past Brenda Heck's house, Squirrel's dying to know if I did sex with her yet. He keeps looking at her house and then goes, "Well, did you fuck her?"

"She's a prime piece of ass," says Crow, sitting shotgun. "Betcha ya did."

"That's for me to know and you to find out." *The truth is I haven't. She's a big tease with flirty makeup, big tits and short dresses. She's never even given me a handjob.*

"Merrily we roll along, roll along...!" sings Squirrel.

Squirrel and Crow are fun to hang with. Squirrel is weird and Crow is nutty. *Weird* and *nutty* is their charm. Ever since middle school it was obvious there were a few loose screws in Squirrel's head. He once poured a full bottle of Smirnoff vodka into an empty bowl, refilled the bottle with water, and called out to his grandmother, *"Hey, Snagglepuss! Watch this!"* Then he started guzzling the water. His grandmother laughed with pride *"Ha! You're just like me!"*

In Squirrel's backyard, is a big red barn where we're always looking at *Playboy*, fighting, and talking crap about how life sucks. Recently, he surprised me, saying, *"Pete, I've turned over a new leaf. From now on, I'm gonna be kind, compassionate, and listen to others, and if they don't agree with me, they can go suck my cock."* That's vintage Squirrel. His favorite thing to eat are packets of Domino sugar.

His parents leave Squirrel alone a lot because they both work—or because they're sick and tired of telling him to stop beating up his two younger brothers, or because they're fed up talking to his teachers about his misbehavior, or because they've given up telling him to pick up his dirty underwear off the floor, or because they just want to get away from the awful prick. Squirrel is a barrel of monkeys.

Crow, on the other hand, is a happy-go-lucky kid who lives next to a cornfield with a dirty chicken coop in back. His parents leave him alone, too. His mother doesn't make him brush or floss his teeth, and neither does his father because he's always sitting on a barstool at The Rec. That's why Crow's teeth are sometimes kinda green. It's hard not to notice green teeth.

It's fun hanging out with these guys but it's not intellectually challenging. But maybe that's the point. Hanging with them makes me feel smart?

Now I'm driving past our high school. It's all dark and Squirrel wants to break in. "Let's break a window and crawl inside."

"And do what?" asks Crow.

"I dunno. Mess around."

"That's stupid. You're just plain stupid," says Crow.

"You're the stupid one," barks Squirrel, "and I am *God!*"

"No, stupid, you're High Scum of the Universe!" And we all break out laughing.

We're very good at trash talk. Squirrel's gifted in that area. We *love* ranking on each other. Dabbling in juvenile delinquency, stealing a car, driving around without a license, talking about breaking windows while wearing pajamas is a lot of fun.

Merrily we roll along, roll along...

I look at Squirrel's face in the rear-view mirror. I wonder when he will go to jail. I know he'll end up in prison one day. I wonder what his crime will be.

Like I said, I'm no brilliant genius, but hanging out with these guys is a lot of fun.

The Police

I'm driving down Piermont Road—through Demarest, toward Cresskill. I'm watching my speed, but when I see a big gravel parking lot in front of a restaurant, I get stupid and start doing wheelies. Squirrel and Crow are belly laughing and still ragging on each other. "When I die," says Squirrel, "I wanna be cremated and have my ashes thrown in your face!"

"Oh, yeah? Well, when *I* die…"

That's when I hear a police siren and see red lights flashing.

An hour later, my stepfather, wearing his pajamas, steps into the Cresskill police station. He talks to the cops--probably about how he's a prominent New Jersey politician and a county judge in Lodi, and about me being such a good kid who's never been in trouble with the law.

I'm let go.

Mr. Schizza drives me home, I'm waiting for him to get all loud and shouty. But he doesn't. I appreciate that. But he does set a court date for me to appear in the Hackensack County Court this coming weekend.

I don't know how Crow and Squirrel got home—probably a taxi.

Ironically, the last sentence I remember Squirrel saying was, *Crow, when I die, I want my ashes thrown in your face.* And then Crow going, *Oh, yeah? Well, when I die…*

It's very ironic because they both will die young. The Closter Police found Crow hanging from the rafters in the chicken coop behind his house. And Squirrel was diagnosed as schizophrenic. He was thrown out the army, wandered around the country and his decayed dead body was found in a boxcar down in Florida, or he died up in Boston, depending on who you believe.

120

Let's Pretend I'm Not Stupid

It's the first day of summer school and I'm sitting in Mrs. Frolich's class because I failed algebra. She's handing out the algebra books, saying, "Write your name on the inside front cover..." Frolich isn't pretty or feminine like my mother—but few women are. *(My mother, in the past eight years, has escaped the sweat shops in the garment distrect and has blossomed into successful loungewear designer for Kayser-Roth on Fifth Avenue.)*

Mrs. Frolich isn't ugly, but she could do much better in the looks department. She has short, chopped hair and wears black clunky glasses, and you should see her dress—gray and peach diagonal stripes. *Very unappealing,* my mother would whisper. Mrs. Frolich is all math, numbers, and equations, and hasn't cracked a smile all morning. There doesn't seem to be much poetry to this woman.

Mr. Colantoni, our stubby principal, just walked in the room, frowning..."You all have failed—that's why you're here. Mrs. Frolich is a *teacher*—not a *policeman*. She will not tolerate any tomfoolery. You will arrive to class on time and be in your seat when the bell rings. You will raise your hand and wait for her to call on you. You will not chew gum. If you cannot control yourself, *I* will. Do we understand each other?" Then he looks directly at me. "If you are disruptive in any way, I will expel you. Is that understood?" Then he stomps out. Okay, Colantoni might've suspended me a few times for fighting and skipping school, but I don't think I deserved his abusive stare. *Do you?*

Mrs. Frolich now goes, "Open your books to page 8 and complete equations 1—10." But what she really means is: *Shut, the fuck, up and do your work.*

After an hour of *Shut, the fuck, up and do your work,* Mrs. Frolich picks up a piece of chalk writes on the board:

$$X-7 = x/3 + 4."$$

121

Numbers start crawling around the inside of my skull--they're upside down and backwards and all jumbled up. Who ever invented algebra should be shot. I hope with all my heart there will be no algebra up in heaven.

"Now," says Frolich, "there will be a brief 10-minute break. If you find yourself struggling and feeling frustrated that's a *good* sign. That means you're *learning* and on your way to comprehension."

My friend, Abe Abrahamsen, and I are standing at the urinal, draining the vein. He goes, "*If you find yourself struggling and feeling frustrated…*"

"*…that's a good sign!*" I laugh.

Me and Emile

Frolich has assigned us 40 linear equations for homework. The problem is there's no desk at dad's house so I'm lying here on the carpet looking up at my idol, Emile Griffith.

You sure you wanna be boxer? says Emile.

"Yes, sir."

Well, try knocking out your 40 linear equations first.

But I just can't concentrate... *Brenda is moaning as I finger her pussy...Coach Sgro is called me a happy horse-shit...my dad's asking, if I'm practicing the saxophone...my brother is wearing my mother's purple caftan...Gram is getting drunk...* **Monkey mind.** *A magician pulls a rabbit out of his hat easier than I can pull out the answer of a linear equation from my brain.*

Why can't I concentrate? Have I eaten too many paint chips at dad's cottage? Am I taking too many shots to the head? Was I born stupid?...*Right now I have a wicked boner thinking about Brenda moaning with her eyes closed and jaw jutting out...*

Mrs. Frolick said: *If you find yourself struggling and feeling frustrated that's a good sign. That means you're learning and on your way to comprehension...* After a while, I start to concentrate—Brenda, Coach Sgro, Gram, Emile Griffith, and my father fade away and it clicks--me and the math.

At the end of the summer semester, my report card arrives in the mail...**A+.**

By the way, if you're wondering, **X-7 = x/3 + 4...** The answer is **X=3**

Thank you very much, Mrs. Frolich. You're a great teacher.

Where Do I Fit In?

It's period 6 in Mr. Chase's social studies class and we're watching this black and white documentary about a Congolese tribe. Barefoot hunters are running through the jungle, naked women are building grass huts, fishermen are standing in a muddy river holding spears. Farmers are digging and women are cooking. Everyone fits in somewhere. I'm sorta watching, but not really. I'm worrying about *me*—where will I fit into American society? I'm always thinking these anxious, worrisome thoughts and I'm always coming up with anxious, worrisome answers.

A Career Aptitude Test

Yesterday in Mr. Dahlgren's science class we took a fun test. He said, "Some people give more thought choosing which pair of socks to wear in the morning than in choosing their life's occupation. So, this morning you will take an aptitude test designed to open your eyes to various career pathways awaiting you in the future."

The questions were like this:

1) *Where would you live if you could live anywhere in the world?*

    a) *Where I live now*

    b) *By the ocean or in the mountains*

    c) *Everywhere and anywhere*

    d) *New York or Hollywood*

2) *Select one word that best fits you:*

    a) *Risk-taker*

    b) *Cautious*

    c) *Stable*

    d) *Original*

Some questions were like this:

Rate each statement according to how well it describes you

    Inaccurate   Neutral   Accurate

I make friends easily.

I have a vivid imagination.

I love large parties.

I trust others.

I use flattery to get ahead.

I feel others' emotions.

I see beauty in things others don't.

The test results came back today with careers like *Accountant, Engineer, Sales Representative, Travel Agent, Nurse, Dog Groomer.* The career that suited me best was *Forest Ranger.*

"Nothing wrong with forest ranger," smiles Mr. Dahlgren.

"I guess," I go.

"It's an important occupation, saving the environment."

"Don't get me wrong, Mr. Dahlgren. I can like a tree. But I don't think it would give me much joy. There's not much status walking around trees all day wearing a brown uniform. And the money probably sucks."

"You will find your way, Peter."

I hope someday I'll find my place in society. My parents found theirs—a songwriter, a clothes designer, a lawyer. *Me—a professional boxer?*

I wonder if Gram ever found her place in society. She's driving to the bar in town and is coming home drunk too many times. And David aint finding his way. I'll tell you more about my lovely brother in the next chapter.

Oh, David

Last August David enrolled in Long Island University, in Brooklyn, but dropped out. David has a bad habit of dropping out. Like I said. he quit everything—piano lessons, trumpet lessons, the Boy Scouts. Our parents bought him a puppy but he refused to clean up after it, so we got rid of it. He quit mowing the lawn. He quit the football team, and he's never had a long-term girlfriend. He quit when I punched him down in the basement. David has the reputation as the best pool player in Closter, but when money's on the table, he crumbles.

David's a quitter.

After dropping out of college, he enlisted in the navy, but quit that, too...*drugs*

This past summer, he married a big-titted brunette named Judy. (Remember I told you a few chapters ago about Joe, the boy David tied up in a tree?) Well, big-titted Judy is Joe's nineteen-year-old sister. She and David spent their honeymoon in Greenwich Village. While high on heroin, David plowed my mother's purple Firebird into a bread truck on Houston Street. The car was totaled, Judy's two front teeth were knocked out, and David's jaw was fractured in three places. They spent the night at St. Vincent's Hospital

Now they're back home, sitting at the kitchen table--the same kitchen table where I chucked a fat meatball into David's ear.

"How you guys doing?" I go.

Judy opens her mouth and lisps, "Pretty, aint I?" Her bloody gums and the gaping hole where her front teeth used to be, is not pretty. David doesn't say anything because his jaw is wired shut.

Wait, it gets better...

David on the Floor

David and Judy have now moved into a rented on Demarest Avenue, the west side of Closter. One afternoon, Judy opens the bathroom door and sees David naked on the floor next to the toilet bowl with a needle sticking in his arm.

He's rushed to the Pascack Valley Hospital and is declared DOA, which means, *dead on arrival.*

Doctors work on him--and just like Vinny's overdose a year ago--they bring him back to life.

*****

David, what's WRONG with you? You are my big brother! Why are you so emotionally unstable? Why are you shooting heroin into your fucking veins? I wish you could see yourself the way everyone sees you—you are smart and handsome, and your family loves you. You have money and a good education and food is on your table. Lots of people have it worse off than you.

Even though I'm not shooting heroin into my veins, I realize the pool table down in the basement of The Rec has been asking me the same questions. *Pete, what's wrong with you? Why are you so emotionally unstable? Why can't you see yourself like other people do?*

...Am I gonna end up hurting myself, like David?

Heroin and Boxing

My life is slowly coming into focus--David and I are both sick--he's shooting heroin and I'm fighting. We both are nice and shiny on the outside—we have good table manners, floss our teeth at night, and we coexist at the Schizzas well enough. But inside we're a hot mess. The big difference is he does drugs and I throw punches.

I'm not a psychologist, I'm only a junior in high school, but I think David has a severe inferiority complex. I might have one, too, but I'm not willing to admit it. I looked up *"inferiority complex"* in the dictionary and it said *"an intense personal feeling of inadequacy, often resulting in the belief that one is in some way deficient, or inferior, to others."*

If I'm gonna be fighting in Madison Square Garden and win the middleweight title, I better not have an inferiority complex.

But, yeah, I think I might.

My First Amateur Fight is Next Week

So, anyway, I'm gonna be a senior in a few months and I'm hoping to get my first amateur fight--a real boxing match inside a ring with ropes, a bell, and judges. I can't wait.

Each day after school, I've been driving to Bufano's Gym in Jersey City. Each day my palms sweat on the steering wheel and I chew the skin inside my cheek. By the time I hit Kennedy Boulevard my testicles are shriveling up. I hate when that happens.

Pete, you're not scared—you're just nervous.

I park on the corner of Beacon and Oakland and ignore my squirming testicles as I walk up the twenty nine steps to the gym. I'm forgetting about David--he can hurt himself with heroin, if he wants. Me, I prefer to hurt other people, rather than myself.

As I enter the gym I'm forgetting about inferiority complexes because I don't have one.

Everyone Is Rabid

Bufano's Gym is a stink. It's a thudding noise…a quality of strength…a pit…a moan…a light…a dream…a perfect poem. It's an ancient gymnasium where dry plaster falls from the ceiling on to your shoes. Zoological smells and flabby brown odors float through the air. It's not a clean gym and I don't go barefoot, especially when showering. *(I gotta be honest—I stole some of those words from John Steinbeck in a book we read in Mrs. Simon's class.)*

Inside, sweaty fighters are panting as they thump and thwack heavy bags. Dark men shadowbox in dirty mirrors and a bald lady grunts as she spars. Everyone seems rabid. At the end of the round, Eddie Parks, a promising welterweight from Paterson, lets loose a spine-tingling primal scream. It's a gym violently perfect—hot, humid, and loud with grunting.

This is exactly where I wanna be. Even though the first week I shit my pants walking up the stairs.

So You Wanna Fight?

"So you wanna fight?" goes Dom Bufano.

"Yes, s-sir."

He's sitting at a round wooden table and flips his *Daily News* shut. "Ever fight before?"

"No." I want to appear tough, but not *too* tough, because I don't want him expecting too much from me. I don't reveal my fighting history: 20 street fights...me knocking out 23-year-old Richie Ugles in his basement, his head hitting the Maytag washing machine before dropping to the floor...or about me dropping muscular Iggy McPartland with all his tattoos...or about me holding my own against my three older brothers down in the basement...or me brawling with my stepfather and getting the best of the bastard. *(I'm not credentialing myself as a tough guy here because I'm really not.)*

"Where you from?" asks Dom.

"Closter."

He grins and I know *exactly* what he's thinking. *Here comes another soft white kid from Bergen County.* He's not seeing an under-privileged black boy who needs to fight his way out of the Jersey City ghetto. He knows full well *nobody* boxes who doesn't have to. But he *is* seeing a mixed-up kid who *needs* to box. He's seeing a teenager with a scream inside him that he can't explain—a confused kid who feels alive when punching a bag. I know that sounds sick,but it's the truth. Show me a fighter and I'll show you a sick bastard.

"I came to f-fight," I say.

He squints with his one good eye. "Why?"

"W-Why? Cuz I wanna enter the Gloves, that's why."

He looks me up and down like I'm a slab of beef. His gimpy left eye is giving me the willies. "You about seventy pounds?"

"One hundred and sixty five."

"Okay," he nods, "ya can move around with some of my boys and we'll see what ya got."

"Thank you, Mr. Bufano." I drop my blue duffle bag and we shake hands.

"What did ya say your name was?"

"Pete Wood."

"Okay, Woods—boxing's a tough job, but somebody's gotta do it. I guess that's why you're here. Just so you know--if anybody can make you into a fighter, it's me."

"When do I get a f-fight?"

"Next week there's a smoker."

"What's that?"

"Unofficial bout. Won't go on your record. I'll find you an inexperienced Jew for ya." He grins.

Dom seems like a pretty nice guy, but his damaged eye creeps me out. Probably got thumbed? Hope that never happens to me. And I hope he's not another Coach Sgro who treats a kid like dirt hoping *he'll grow flowers*. I love that line—it's from an e.e.cummings' poem.

"Treat a man like dirt-he produces flowers."

Another Talk with My Mom

First, let me say this—I never talk to my mother anymore. Yeah, we live in the same house, but that's about it. I try to stay out of every room she's in and I try not to make eye contact with her. I remember when she was my mother and I loved her, but now she's Schizza's wife and I hate her.

Yeah, I guess I might still love her somewhere deep inside me because she's a very good person—but not a very good mother. She has a big heart and always means well, but ever since I got trapped living with this new family, she goes her way and I go mine.

*****

I'm punching the heavy bag when she walks down into the basement, sits on the steps, and smiles at me. "Peter, I don't like the idea of you spending so much time down here alone. Why don't you come upstairs and join the rest of the family."

"Not now."

I know my mother wants more for me than punching a heavy bag down in the basement. If you glimpse at her pretty face , you'd never guess last month David was in a hospital recovering from a heroin overdose. Her face, all make-uped up, always looks like a photo in *Glamour Magazine.* I'm sure she still feels terrible guilt about David, but you'd never know it. Her life has not skipped a beat. She's still driving to work, still smiling, still eating gourmet food at White Beaches Country Club with her rookie state representative. I guess, in her own way, she's very strong. But she'll never worm her way into my heart no matter how hard she tries.

"Come up and watch *The Man from Uncle* with us," she goes. "There's ice cream cake waiting for you upstairs. Gram will cut you a big slice."

"Not now."

I don't mean to be a dickhead, but I have so little feeling for this woman, and she has so little understanding of me. She thinks hitting a bag in the basement is something a smelly cretin does in a dark cave—not her handsome son directly below her well-appointed bedroom.

"Peter, I don't think it's a very good idea you driving to Jersey City to box perfect strangers."

"Yeah, okay."

"I don't like the idea of someone punching my son's head."

"Yeah, okay."

I know I'm dead wrong hating my mother, but what kid doesn't hate his mother every now and then? Maybe someday I'll allow myself to *like* her.

Right now she's yapping at me about school, education, intelligence, and me improving my vocabulary. I've heard it all before. In a minute she's gonna say: *Peter, people tend to live at the level of their language.*

But she and I have different definitions of *language*. Her definition involves me growing into a businessman with a necktie wrapped around my neck and wearing a pinstriped suit which, honestly, reminds me of a man wearing a fucking Squirrel on his back.

"Peter," she says, "you know, people tend to live at the level of their language."

"Screw you! My language is punching! I never stutter when I punch!" is what I wanna say, but don't. I turn my back and continue training for my upcoming smoker. I'm getting pretty good at improving my boxing language. A fighter's intelligence isn't in words.

A voice whispers from my boxing glove.

Boxing is an art—a form of theater

where nobody speaks a foolish word all night—

at least in the ring.

"I'll have Gram save you a big slice when you come up."

"Close the door," I say.

I continue punching and wonder how can she be happy living in this sick house.

The Smoker

Country Village Playground…I'm standing behind a referee who's taking his own sweet time climbing up to the ring. *Hurry up, ref! I've been waiting a long time for this!* Honestly, I'm more excited than scared. What could be more exciting for a kid fighting in a ring? It's assault and battery with 10-ounce gloves.

My opponent is Jamaal Brown from Brooklyn. Judging from his black face, he's not Jewish and I'm sure he wants to kick my white ass. But I don't give a rat's ass if he's Muhammad Ali or Joe Frazier. I've run so many miles and sparred so many rounds, I'm gonna whup him.

The bell rings and we start tearing into each other. I'm not afraid of blood clots, asthma, or cowardice which I know are all inside me.

I'm exactly where I wanna be—fighting in a ring.

I won't bore you with the details except we are like two graceless Neanderthals throwing rocks at each other. After three rounds, and a lot of thumping and smashing, my hand is raised in the air--a winner by split decision.

After the fight, a young boy—*and I'll never forget this*--runs up to me with a pen and paper. "Wow, Mister! You're an *animal*! Can I have your autograph?"

I'm an animal! *Music to my ears! Maybe there is a bit of jackdempsey in me?*

"Sure," I say, signing my name.

Mr. Steelman's Drama Class

I'm a senior now and I have learned to become comfortably uncomfortable in school. It's true I'm a second-string student—but a first-string athlete in baseball and football. I'm 17 years old and no longer suck my thumb or wet the bed, but I still stutter and scramble around for the right words all the time.

What helps me is that I'm starting halfback and score my fair share of touchdowns. But Coach Sgro still treats me like dirt.

There's no more *Peter Wood Fan Club*, but that's totally okay. Even though I stew in anxiety every day, I'm beginning to actually like myself, and my *Fuck-Me-Disease* is beginning to fade. A big part of that is *sports* and being lucky enough to have a tough coach like Sgro and smart teachers who push me.

Mrs. Tsaggos, Mr. Colantoni's secretary, recently said, "Peter, we never see you in the principal's office anymore—you must be cleaning up your act." That's because I'm not fighting--at least in school anymore.

In the last two paragraphs I've tried to point out that, believe it or not, I've become a decent student.

My favorite class is drama. We don't perform on stage, but we do read aloud. *Death of a Salesman* and *Antigone* were fun, and today it was very cool when Mr. Steelman asked, "Peter, would you like to read the part of Nick in *Who's Afraid of Virginia Woolf*? He's an ex-boxer. "

Normally, I never miss a good opportunity to shut up in class, but I go, "S-Sure." My *Fuck-Me Disease* is fading!

I happen to be a pretty good *second-string* reader, but I'm always self-conscious and look at myself through other people's eyes when I read. *Wow! Peter's reading so slooow! Peter's not reading with the proper emotional tone and inflection. Listen to him st-stutter!*

Basically, that last paragraph is what it's like in my head most days. So, yeah, it's still an awful mess in there.

I read the boxer part today and give myself a B-.

What Do You Most Strive For?

Yeah, Mr. Steelman's drama class is pretty cool. I like when he asks us *self-examination questions.* Last week, before reading *Antigone,* he goes, *Which sex has it easier in our society?* We all started arguing—especially Robert Hershan, who, I know for a fact, is gonna be an arguey lawyer one day.

Before reading *Of Mice and Men,* Mr. Steelman asked, *If you could increase your I.Q. by 40 points by having an ugly scar stretching from your mouth to your eye, would you do so?* Most of us boys said *yes* and *all* the girls said *no. Figures.*

Mr. Steelman says, *These questions seem silly but they're really about serious topics like love, money, integrity, generosity, pride, and death. You might even find these questions dangerous or painful, but they can help start you on a path of self-illumination and personal growth.*

How can a question be dangerous?

Today's question is this: *What do you most strive for in your life: accomplishment, security, love, power, excitement, knowledge, or something else?* The class goes silent…then responds.

"Love," says, Linda D'Amico.

"Accomplishment," says Robert Hershan.

"Knowledge," says Cindy Yost.

"Happiness," says Diane Di Blasio.

"Yes, Diane," says Mr. Steelman, "but what *gives* you your happiness?"

"I guess *love?*" she says.

Steelman looks at me. "How about you, Peter?"

140

I shrug. "Leave me alone, Mr. Steelman," is what I want to say, but don't.

*****

That night in bed, I get thinking about Mr. Steelman's question. I wanted to say *I strive for status*—which is true. But, secretly I strive for something much deeper. I'm ashamed to admit it, but deep down, I strive for *security*. The security I feel with my dad--the comfort I feel eating a Swanson TV Dinner with him at his dinner table, or watching *Twilight Zone* with him on the couch, or driving to Carvel with him for a chocolate ice cream cone with sprinkles. Dad *always* orders the *Pecan Tree* with vanilla ice cream.

Football Practice Sucks

It's a cold and rainy November day outside and Coach Sgro is busting our balls. *You're all happy horse shits! You guys should be ashamed of yourselves! You stink!* We're completely captive to this madman. We're supposed to *eat—drink—and shit football.* He even expects us to *sleep* with a football. *Fuckin' idiot.*

Sgro sucks the fun out of football with shitty tackling and hitting drills over and over and over again—*Work! Work! Work! Fatigue makes cowards of us all!* I'm gonna quit the next time he yells *It's my way or the highway or* calls us *Happy horse shits.* But it's a great feeling when a packed stadium cheers for you after you worked so hard and did something good. So, just forget what I said about quitting.

In the locker room, at the end of practice, Crow, my meat-gun sparring partner, goes, "You hear about Brenda?"

"She's moving to Montgomery," I go.

"Is she taking her jiggly tits with her?" asks Squirrel.

This past weekend, Brenda and me were watching the George Chuvalo—Dante Cane fight on *The Wide World of Sports* in my bedroom. We were lying on my pull-out sofa and she was slowly stroking my naked belly with her hand. That always makes my cock quiver. I *love* when she makes my cock quiver. But petting my belly was all she did! Coach Sgro might be a ballbuster, but Brenda is a cock teaser. That's worse.

I realize that last paragraph isn't doing me any favors. It makes me look like an ugly sexist pig who only thinks about sex, screwing girls, and big tits. That's only half true.

THE GOLDEN GLOVES

The Center of the Universe

Golden Gloves Sign-Up

All us tough guys are lined up in the *Daily News* Building on 220 East 2nd Street waiting to get our physical and picture taken. No one is smiling or talking much. We're just toughing it out. Stoic assholes. *Stoic* is a new word I learned. It means *calm and without showing emotion, a person who can endure pain or hardship.*

I'm keeping my face blank like an emotionless psychopath—just like Sonny Liston, the former heavyweight champion--except I'm white.

There are only a few white guys standing on line--most are black or Spanish. And all sizes—heavyweights, middleweights, and flyweights. We're all standing here being tough, but everyone's palms I bet are all sweaty—especially a small group of flyweights clowning around trying to convince us they're not scared stiff. *(Wouldn't it be ironic if one of these pricks on line was the same punk who held a knife to my brother's throat when we lived in the city?)*

When it's my turn to sign up, I grab a pen with my right hand and sign in righty. *(No one needs to know I'm lefty--just like no one needs to know I once sucked my thumb, wet the bed, play the saxophone, have a stamp collection, and stutter.)*

The Golden Gloves official looks at my signature and goes, "That's sloppy writing you got, boy. You illiterate?"

I shrug and walk away. The kid behind me stares. Somehow stepping into a ring with an illiterate psychopath is very unsettling…

Driving to Bufano's Gym

I'm driving down 9W to the gym and inside my monkey-mind I'm watching a grainy, poorly-lit, black-and-white movie... *I'm seeing my mother 12 years ago climbing out her bedroom window...she's running down Closter Dock Road in her negligee...her hair is whipping in the wind and she's crying. She doesn't care about her goddamn hair...she's going insane...*

...I see a cop pulling his squad car up alongside her...he's opening the passenger door and she crawls in...he's escorting her to the Closter police station with his arm wrapped around her...she's put of psychiatric hold.

...I'm turning onto route 46. My blue duffle bag is stuffed with my green nylon trunks, hand-wraps, bag gloves, mouthpiece, jump rope, and towel...*Dom is telling tell me who I'm sparring today. I hope I do good and my front tooth won't get knocked out.*

...Cars are passing me on Kennedy Boulevard...*I'm six years old, walking down Closter Dock Road to play wiffle ball with Paul. A police car is pulling alongside me. The policeman is rolling down his window. "Hello! Are you Peter Wood?"*

"Yes, sir."

"I'm a good friend with your mother. She's a very nice lady. Please say hello to her for me." He's handing me a quarter. I like policemen, but not this one.

These Magical Men

Hooray! Football season is finally over and there's no more insane football or crazy Coach Sgro. Now each day I'm driving to Jersey City--the armpit of the world--to Bufano's which is much more insane and crazy than football. I kid you not.

Pro football players--Jim Brown, Johnny Unitas, Dick Butkus, Deacon Jones—are not crazy or insane--they are comformy athletes smoothed out by college. But pro boxers *are* insane and crazy. They are *non-conformy*. They are street. Sugar Ray Robinson, Emile Griffith, John L. Sullivan, Jack Dempsey, and Rubin "Hurricane" Carter are all outsiders and their aura of nobility and menace captivate me. (The word *aura* is another cool word. I learned it in Mr. Steelman's drama class. It means: *a distinctive atmosphere or quality that seems to surround or be generated by a person, thing, or place.*)

Boxers are magical men with trophy noses and bumpy faces who have chosen for themselves an insane profession.

Now I'm training alongside them! There's light heavyweight Jimmy Dupree, who fought for the light heavyweight crown in Caracas, Venezuela...Marcel Bizien, a grizzled middleweight contender—(his locker is next to mine.) Crazy Otho Tyson, a New Jersey lightweight contender missing a few important teeth...and heavyweight contenders, Brian O'Melia and Chuck Wepner, who fight in Madison Square Garden all the time.

Chuck Wepner is the most famous fighter in here. He's called "The Bayonne Bleeder" for obvious reasons. Early this year Sonny Liston, the ex-heavyweight champion carved up Wepner's face in the Jersey City Armory, giving Wepner 57 stitches over both eyes.

(But Wepner is best known for fighting Muhammad Ali for the heavyweight title in 1975 and knocking Ali down before getting stopped himself in the 15th.)

One year later, Wepner was insane enough to wrestle 520-pound Andre The Giant in Shea Stadium. Wepner looked like a toy when he was tossed over the top rope onto the concrete floor.

*Wepner is also the inspiration for Sylvester Stallone's 1976 Oscar-Winning film Rocky. Stallone's main character, Rocky, **is** Chuck Wepner.*

I idolize these men who have perfected their left hooks and right uppercuts. Their brains are in their fists and their mouths are in their gloves. It's so cool training next to them. If it weren't for Coach Sgro's insane football workouts I would never be able to exist here. *Thanks, Coach.*

I might be lacking technical boxing skill at this point, but that'll change. I'm sparring and learning fast. Each day, my brain is becoming more and more paleo-mammalian. Boxing is becoming my solution to everything--*if life sucks, the answer is boxing.* If I can't think of a word or if I stutter, *boxing is the answer.*

Depressed? Go to the gym.

Angry? Hit the bag.

Full of hate? Spar.

Scared? Do roadwork.

Boxing is better than heroin.

Jimmy Hargrove

Jimmy Hargrove is a middleweight who kicks my ass every day--but he's nice about it. He pulls his punches, and gently beats me up. He pecks my face with swift nimble jabs, and then slams my body with hard hooks. I'm target practice--his valuable sparring partner. That's why he goes easy on me--he doesn't want me to quit. Yeah, he kicks my ass gently and politely.

But with each ass-whupping, I'm getting better.

Jimmy's day-job is cleaning Jersey City school buses, then he comes here to kick my butt. Last year he reached the Golden Gloves finals but lost a close decision. He's so damn good I can hardly hit the bastard. If I come away with a bloody nose, that's totally okay because I'm sharpening my skills.

If you find yourself struggling and feeling frustrated that's a good sign. That means you're learning and on your way to comprehension.

Today, after we spar, I know *exactly* what Jimmy will say—he'll tap the top of my headgear, smile, and go, *"Petey, you gettin' good!"*, even though we both know I suck.

So, today, after sparring three rounds, Dom is taking off my gloves and toweling off my bloody face, and Jimmy, smiles, taps the top of my headgear and goes, *"Petey, you gettin' good!"*

Dom nods. "Is."

There's a special aura here at Bufano's. It's magically turning me into a gentler and more intelligent person. I'm no longer street fighting and I'm getting straight *B*s in school. But honestly, I hate getting beat up. It's very humiliating.

Sure, boxing is an ugly sport. But it's a beautiful ugly.

It's so confusing. Why am I *really* here? Why am I driving an hour to the armpit of the world to get beat up? Why am I putting myself through all this bullshit?

Why? Like I said earlier, I don't like to think too deep.

But I'm slowly discovering something weird. I'm leading *three* separate lives all at once—*a public life...a private life...and a secret life.*

"See ya tomorrow?" asks Jimmy.

"Okay," I smile. That's my *public self.*

Nathalie and Guy Meet--1947

I'm driving to the gym, down route 46, when inside my skull I'm watching another grainy, black-and-white movie about my family...

... I'm seeing my mother, 18-year-old beauty queen wearing fluffy white earmuffs at Wollman Rink in Central Park. She spots a mature 35-year-old man skating, and whispers to her girlfriend, "That's the man I'm going to marry."

Within a year, they tie the knot. Nathalie Pierce now becomes Nathalie Wood--and she looks just like Natalie Wood, the movie star—only prettier.

*Nathalie is proud of her 35-year-old husband—a successful composer who has recently written a hit song—**My One and Only Love**. And Guy is proud of his young 18-year-old wife--a stunning model dabbling in painting--or a painter dabbling in modeling.*

Shortly, they are blessed with one son...and then another.

But after a few years Nathalie and Guy start arguing. It might be their age difference, or their religious difference, or financial stress, or simple parental pressures. Whatever it is, they vow to work it out and move to Closter, New Jersey.

She's Christian--he's Jewish. They compromise and join a Unitarian church in Oradell to seek marital counseling. During Sunday school, I see me puking up apple cider and a sugar cookie. I know something is wrong—and it's not my stomach...My mother has been fucking the Unitarian minister.

Nathalie and Guy divorce.

Dang! I'm seeing all of this monkey-mind crap in my mind—*My parents arguing...me puking...my brother slumped beside a toilet bowl with a needle sticking in his arm...my father pushing my mother to the ground...my mother crawling out a window...a smiling policeman giving me a quarter...*

...Now I'm gnawing on my mouthpiece as I climb into the ring so Jimmy Hargrove can kick my ass.

*****

I'm driving home to Closter and realize I'm not wanting anything my classmates want—good grades, a senior prom date, or college. I just wanna fight in Madison Square Garden and feel the New York Golden Gloves necklace wrapped around my neck.

In the Dressing Room

St. Jude's High School, the Bronx

I'm in the dressing room for my first Golden Gloves fight. It's just an ordinary classroom in St. Jude's--a blackboard, books, a round clock on the wall.

Dom is giving me instructions and I nod like I'm listening, which I'm not. I'm listening to the Pepsi gurgling in my stomach. I'm trying not to think too much because thinking is dangerous. I'm physically strong, but mentally weak. My muscles are much more reliable than my brain. Instinct is better than thought in a ring, anyway.

If I start thinking, I'd be like, *What are you doing here? You're not a fighter by heredity--your mother and father are peaceful artists from the suburbs.*

But I found out that there's not many things in this world, other than a Hershey candy bar or an orgasm, that have as much instant gratification as one solid left hook to a guy's jawbone.

*****

So now I'm just sitting here in this horrible dressing room, which, as I said, is a high school classroom. There's a rolled-down map of America, a bunch of geography books, and a metal pencil sharpener. I'm sitting here making myself look calm, not wasting energy sneering or scowling, like the idiot next to me chewing his gum like he wants to kill it with his teeth.

But I *do* want to look Cro-Magnon. So I do my best Sonny Liston stare. Liston, a jailbird turned world heavyweight champion had a horrifying baleful stare. Personally, I think the traits that make up an anti-social human being are the same traits that make up a good fighter. It's my educated opinion that you can't be a good fighter if you don't have something wrong with you.

(By the way, *"baleful"* is a word I recently looked up. It means *threatening harm and menacing.)*

Yeah, I'm quickly discovering a dressing room is a very lousy place to be. Everyone's machoing it out while the seconds tick away. You *wait...and...wait* ignoring your fear. You tell yourself you're *nervous*, but what you really are is *scared*. But, honestly, the thought of getting punched in the face hurts much worse than the actual punch, that's why I deaden my mind into a vegetable. *No brain, no pain.*

I stare at the white flecks in my fingernails. How'd they get there? Sweat's sliding down my sides onto my green nylon boxing trunks. Dom always tells me, *Pete, the secret to fighting is maintaining your equilibrium. If you wanna be a fighter, the muscles of your soul gotta be strong.* He's right. I think that goes for life, as well.

My First Golden Gloves Fight

In the corner, Dom's stuffing in my mouthpiece and rubbing my shoulders with Vaseline. I begin flailing my arms overhead, then punching the air above my head which loosens my muscles and gives me a longer reach. Plus, it looks apelike.

Me and Greg Burke walk to the middle of the ring. The referee goes, *Okay, boys, I want a nice clean fight...*Violence is coating Burke's eyeballs because he wants to take me apart...*Shake hands and come out fighting...*I didn't hear a damn word the ref said.

Burke races across the ring and attacks. I crouch, and his punches whistle overhead. I come up with a solid left hook—there's nothing graceful about that punch, but it works because he's lying on the canvas. *"ONE...TWO...THREE..."*

Stay down, I pray.

Dang! He gets up.

Again, he rushes me. He's trying to prove being dropped was a big mistake. It wasn't. I drop him again with another left hook off a jab. He slumps back to the canvas.

"ONE...TWO...THREE...FOUR...FIVE..."

Please! Stay! Down!

He gets up--but not wisely. This time *I* attack. I won't go into detail because it'll sound braggy, but I hammer home a straight right--it's like hitting a guy's head with the meat of a baseball bat. He slumps to the canvas and counted out--his corner man jumps in with smelling salts.

A first round knockout!

Somewhere sitting in the crowd are my dad and stepmother, the woman who sewed the nice big green shamrock on the back of my white terrycloth robe.

I hop out of the ring and strut down the aisle. My high school friends are shouting, "WOOD! WOOD! WOOD!"

"I'M AN ANIMAL!" I keep screaming. The crowd is hollering--which is all great—but most importantly, I want to put the fear of God into my future opponents who might be watching.

"I'M AN ANIMAL!"

Driving home in Dom's car I close my eyes and replay the fight in my head. Every leather-lunged fan loved me tonight.

"You did real good," Dom tells me.

"Thanks, Dom."

My eyes are still closed as we drive through the Holland Tunnel back to Jersey City. I re-play the fight again--this time from my father's perspective. I see worry-lines creasing his forehead and I suspect he's deeply concerned about me.

The Next Day

A clipping from today's *New York Daily News* sports page reads:

Peter Wood, Jersey City school boy, representing Bufano's Gym, was one of the most impressive bombers thus far. Wood packs a potent left hook. He flashed it three times in the opening round to topple Greg Burke from Hastings, N.Y. The time was 1:35.

Dang! I never heard such applause in all my life like last night. Everyone was yelling and screaming for *me!* They liked me and it feels great to be liked.

*****

Back here at school, kids are going:

What's it like to knock someone out?

Were you scared?

When are you fighting again? I wanna go!

I like all this attention. And I'm beginning to feel a little *jackdempsey-ish.*

My next fight is next week.

Mimi

Love rushes over me the first time I see beautiful Mimi, a petite junior who is *terrifyingly* gorgeous. We are sitting in the school cafeteria talking for the very first time and my heart is pounding.

"Congratulations on your fight." she goes.

"Thanks." But then I shut up because shutting up is the perfect technique to avoid stuttering. Mimi is doing all the talking and I'm doing all the listening—but, I'm not really listening because I'm too busy looking at her *gorgeousness*. I swear to God, she's the most beautiful girl in school—probably the most beautiful girl on the planet--probably the most beautiful creature ever born.

I bet traffic slows down to look at her face. I've never felt this passionate about a girl before—not even with Brenda, the sexpot with big jiggly tits. "Mimi, I just want to sit here and look at you, if that's okay with you," is what I'm thinking.

Passion is a complicated thing to describe. You can't say it's three feet long and two feet wide, or weighs ten pounds, or it's soft pink, or sounds like a flute, or smells like perfume. Passion is just a hard stiff boner.

Mimi puts her elbows on the table, leans forward, and cups her cheeks with her hands, and says, "Peter, you're nice."

"T-That's my inner beauty," I joke.

She giggles and it seems to travel right down to my belly.

My palms and feet are, of course, sweating. I look away and flex my hands. They're stiff and sore from my fight.

"I must be honest, Mimi, you scare the hell out of me." I don't say that either.

Floyd Patterson, the former Heavyweight Champion of the World, who hid away in dark subway tunnels, once said, *Being in love with a woman, she can be unfaithful, she can be mean, she can be cruel, but it doesn't matter. If you love her, you want her, even though she can do you all kinds of harm.*

I'm looking at Mimi and sweating like before a fight. *Can she do me harm?*

When No One Is Watching

"You are who you are when no one's watching."--that's Coach Sgro whispering inside my head. That is why:

...I always sprint hard, even though he's not watching.

...I always punch the bags in Bufano's fast and hard, even when Dom is watching another fighter.

...I always wipe my piss off the toilet seat in the bathroom, even though my stepfather isn't watching.

...I always brush and floss my teeth every night, even though Gram isn't watching.

...I always say my nightly prayers, even though my mom isn't watching.

...I always avoid watching *The Three Stooges*, even though my dad isn't watching.

...I always avoid cheating on school tests, even when my teacher isn't watching—*well, sometimes I cheat in math.*

"Pete, the muscles of your soul gotta be strong." *whispers* Dom Bufano inside my head. That is why...

...I always drive five days a week to his gym to get my head kicked in by Jimmy.

...I always tell myself I'm not scared even though I am.

...I always tell myself that if boxing is a sickness, it's a healthy sicknesses.

...I always avoid smoking weed or drink at Squirrel's parties, even though a cold Budweiser would taste awfully good.

…I always avoid spending too much time kissing and petting beautiful Mimi. Sex is very dangerous for a future Golden Gloves champion.

…I always avoid masturbating. (Somehow, I'm able to gulp back my wet dreams.)

I bet Jack Dempsey gulped back his wet dreams, too.

A Cauldron of Anger, Youth, and Talent

Okay, so in December I signed up for The Gloves. Gram shook her head at the dinner table and said, *You're nuts! What's so great about coming home with black eyes?*

Sports Illustrated magazine explains it best:

> **The New York Golden Gloves is a brutal tournament—a cauldron of anger, youth, and talent. It started in 1927 by Paul Gallico of the Daily News and has launched the boxing careers of the toughest athletes in sports' history— Sugar Ray Robinson, Floyd Patterson, Jose Torres, Emile Griffith.** (And later Mike Tyson.)

Every young thug in New York City who is good with his hands wants to be a Golden Gloves champ--I'm one of them, even though I'm not a thug, or live in New York City. *(Dom is sneaking me in by using his Jersey City address—which is totally illegal.)*

My mom says: *Peter, I don't like the idea of you getting injured. A head is not meant to be hit.*

My dad says: *Well, lad, I won't stop you if this is what you really want to d-do.*

My brother scoffs: *Good luck, but you're gonna get your ass whipped.*

Mimi says: I can't wait to see your next bout!

My friends at school are like: *This is so cool! I'm buying a ticket for your next fight!*

Gram says: You're not boxing—you're wrestling. You're — wrestling with who you are.

By the way, I looked up the word *cauldron* in the school library. A cauldron is *a large metal pot with a lid and handle used for cooking food over the fire.* I'm not sure how that relates to boxing.

Holy Cross High School, Flushing, New York

I'm sitting in the dressing room for my second Golden Gloves fight—another ordinary high school classroom with a blackboard, desks, and a human skeleton standing in the corner. I count the square tiles on the floor, then trace the blackboard with my eyes over and over again.

I'm, kinda like, suffering because I don't feel like I wanna hit anybody tonight. I'm, kinda like, in trouble because I'm feeling like a soft little mushroom.

My English teacher, Mrs. Simon once said, *Suffering is a noble thing. It teaches a person about life.* Well, I'm sitting here suffering my ass off, and as far as I'm concerned, suffering is overrated. It's not teaching me a damn thing.

I'm looking at all these ugly kids with street-corner faces. They're all, basically, human beings, but I think we're somehow out of whack. I think we're all sadder and sicker than we realize.

One kid with a hair-pick sticking out of his afro is wearing a soiled tee-shirt with **GHETTO UNIVERSITY** written on it.

I doubt if any of us, would have signed up for this ridiculous tournament if some minor tragedy had not twisted our brains out of their natural orbit. Show me a fighter and I'll show you an unhappy childhood.

Guys are taking naps, listening to music, and pacing the floor. Me, I'm counting floor tiles. We're all escaping in our own way. One fighter is playing cards with his trainer, violently slapping the cards down on the table. One kid is rocking back and forth in his chair like he's autistic. No one is playing Parcheesi, Cribbage, or reading a book.

"WOOD!...LET'S GO!"

We're close to fight time. Dom's fitting a brown 12-ounce glove onto my hand, and goes, "Relax, Pete."

"I am relaxed."

"No you aint--you're burpin' and yawnin'."

"So?"

"That's nerves. Wepner's a burper and yawner, too."

"WOOD!...LET'S GO!"

Hearing my name is a mixture of dread and relief. I walk out the dressing room and down the aisle to the ring.

"Wood! Wood! Wood!" chant my high school friends who came to see me knock somebody out.

I climb into the ring but I don't wanna fight. *Where's that scream inside me?*

"Wood! Wood! Wood!"

What's missing? There's no jackdempsey in me. I'm a hair in my own fucking eye.

The Fight

My second fight is another good one. I won't go into detail because it's disrespectful. But tonight I kick Raphael Carr's butt. Real quick I knock him down twice with two left hooks. All I need is one more knockdown and I win by a first round TKO. His mouth is hanging open, he's backpedaling, and he's in bad shape. *One more punch-- just one...* I lunge in with a hook, he arches back, and I miss by an inch. That's when our shoes collide and we stumble through the ropes onto the ring apron.

Intimidation is big in boxing, so since I'm lying on top of him with my face inches away, I open my mouth and growl. Very nonverbal. I just twist my face and snarl. Everyone is yelling, the referee is prying me away, and flashbulbs are exploding. *Total chaos.*

Ding!

"Tryin' to get disqualified?" yells Dom back in the corner.

"Tripped."

"*Don't* trip!" he barks, jamming in my mouthpiece.

Ding!

The referee should never have let Carr continue. I start hammering him. It feels so *nice*, like I'm smashing windows or something. I knock him out in 20 seconds.

That's when the crowd starts booing...*ME!* I can't believe it! I have just given these blood-thirsty bastards exactly what they wanted— they were glued to the violence—and now they're booing! What the fuck? *(I'm not making this shit up. See for yourself on the back page of the Daily News on February 27, 1971.)*

165

Calm Down, Son!

The crowd continues booing *ME*--just because I tripped on my opponent's shoe? *Fuck them!* James J. Corbett, the heavyweight champ back in 1892 was right about a boxing crowd. When he defeated John L. Sullivan for the championship, he realized the very people cheering for him would be the same people booing him if he had lost.

Happiness, anger, and hate are spasming inside me and I feel I'm going mental. The truth is I *am*. I run over to Dom and plant a big fat kiss on his forehead.

"What da fuck you doin'?"

"Fanning the flame!"

The crowd is now booing louder! That's *exactly* what I want! My eyes are bugging out and I'm laughing as I run to the center of the ring and flip the bird to every single asshole. It doesn't make much sense because I'm still wearing my gloves—but they're getting the message.

I *hate* them, and I *love* hating them. At the top of my lungs I'm screaming, "Fuck you! Fuck you!" I hope the other middleweights are watching me go insane. I want them to dread stepping in the ring with *Irish Pete Wood!*

The bell is clanging and the Gloves officials are yelling, "Calm down, son! Calm down!" Dom's going, "They're gonna disqualify you!" The crowd is shrieking. Yeah, there's a lot more shit where it came from—ten years of shit living with the Schizzas—just waiting to explode.

I'm going *canine* jumping around the ring. They should put me on a leash on me.

Yeah, I hope you other middleweights are watching me. You might come from the ghetto, but I AM a ghetto—a walking, breathing, screaming ghetto from suburban Closter, New Jersey!

I'm the One to Beat

After I knock out Carr my dad is waiting for me in the hallway wearing a *worrywart* expression—staring at me like I'm something zoological.

"Hi, Dad."

"Are you o-okay, lad?"

"I'm fine."

"When I watched you tonight, I didn't see my son--I saw someone else."

I'm combing my sweaty hair with my fingers. "It's all an act, Dad. I'm okay."

But am I? Some people walk around with walking pneumonia and don't know it—or have cancer and don't know it. I might be in the middle of a nervous breakdown and don't know it.

I'm looking at Dad's worrywart face and think I'm attracted to fighting because I don't ever wanna grow up to be that worrywart face. *Does that make sense?*

But I have learned to see past his worry and see an insecure ten-year-old boy growing up in Manchester, England whose father absconded on him. I see a *bloke* who smiles and kisses me every time he picks me in his white Valiant on weekends.

Just being with my dad is a luxury because the rest of the time I'm living with strangers. For ten years living with the Schizzas, I've felt like a black dog being raised by white hogs--that's abnormal. Me fighting in this crazy tournament might be abnormal, but an abnormal reaction to an abnormal situation is not abnormal behavior. That's what I think.

*****

168

A black man wearing a black leather jacket runs up to me, shakes my hand, and goes, "Man, you some fighter! You jus' like my idol, Muhammad Ali!" Then he races down the corridor. I notice a strained smile in my dad's worrywart face.

Just then, Dad points to the *GHETTO UNIVERSITY* kid and whispers, "*Blimey!* That chap got clobbered! Herb Goings clobbered him! I hope you don't fight Herb G-Goings."

Please stop worrying, Dad! Something in my mind is starting to gel—something I'd been hoping for...*confidence.*

Don is right--I'm gonna win this tournament. They'd better dread me because I'm the one to beat. The only person who can beat me is **me.**

But first I have to stop hating myself.

Gram

Gram is cooking meatloaf, but meat, breadcrumbs, and a cracked egg are scattered on the floor by her feet. She's hunched over, eyes half closed, squishing the remaining ingredients into a bowl.

"Gram, you okay?"

She ignores me because she's drunk. I'm watching as a string of snot begins dangling...dangling...dangling down from the tip of her nose until it drops into the meatloaf. She doesn't even realize it because she is far, far, far away.

(I know I haven't spoken too much about Gram. That's because she stays hidden. She does all the work around here and is the invisible glue that holds everything together. She never asks much in return, except a little respect, which I'm sure she never gets. It's total wrongness that we all take her for granted. I know I do.)

While I watch Gram squish snot into our meatloaf, I know she's back years ago in West Springfield, Massachusetts, preparing meatloaf for her youngest daughter, Mary Ruth...who will never eat it.

The Mary Ruth Story is a doozy—*doozy* is Gram's word-but I'd use the word *tragic...*

The Mary Ruth Story

After our meatloaf dinner, Gram is watching her favorite television show, *The Red Skelton Hour*. I'm sitting beside her on the white leather sofa massaging her hand, tugging each finger one by one. Her other hand is holding an unfilted Pall Mall.

"Red's funny," she says.

"Too slapsticky," I moan.

"He makes me laugh."

"Gram," I say, "tell me about Mary Ruth."

She takes a long pull on her cigarette. "After Red."

Gram begins the *Mary Ruth Story:* "We owned a farmhouse with oh so many lovely trees in the backyard. My three younguns--Wes, your mother, and Mary Ruth--loved climbing those trees—especially the big elm with heavy limbs and boughs. So, one day I called an arborist."

"Arborist?"

"A man who cuts and removes dead or decaying parts of a tree."

"Tree surgeon?"

She nods, inhales another lungful of smoke, starts coughing, and cigarette ash falls to the floor...

Call Mary Ruth in for Supper

…"I told him, *Please check every tree—particularly that big elm.* When he returned after his inspection, he said, *Mrs. Pierce, everything's hunky dory.* I asked, *How about that elm?* He said, *Healthy as a horse!*

I know where this story is going…

"A few months later, I told Wes, since he was the oldest, *Call Mary Ruth in for supper.* Wes came back into the kitchen and said he couldn't find her, so I told him to look again. He finally found his little sister lying beneath the elm. A rotten bough fell on her head and crushed her skull."

Poor Gram is telling me this story without sighing, crying, or anything. She's just smoking her cigarette and staring at the wall. The story has taken no more than one minute to tell, but I'm sure Mary Ruth is with Gram forever.

I'm still massaging her hand and go, "I'm so sorry, Gram."

"But there's more…," she says, puffing. "A month after Mary Ruth was buried, the arborist killed himself."

Another cigarette ash fell to the floor.

Tell Me about Your Family

I'm driving beautiful Mimi to the County Manor Rehabilitation and Healthcare Center on County Road in Tenafly--she's a candy striper. That's what they call a nurse's helper.

Mimi says, "You never talk about your family."

I shrug.

"Why not?"

I shrug again.

"You're a real chatterbox, aren't you?"

I shrug.

"We can't get married if we don't talk about important stuff, like our families."

"Get m-married?"

She smiles. "You never know!"

"Mimi, I don't wanna talk about family, or my brother, or stepsisters, or stepbrothers, or half-sisters, or marriage. I must be honest, I *do* think the secret to a long and happy marriage is to never get married in the first place." Is what I'm thinking.

"Peter, we need to know if we are compatible. Tell me *something* about them."

"Who?"

"Your *family!*"

"There's a lot of wrongness in my family."

"*Wrongness* isn't a word," she says.

"It should be."

Since *The Mary Ruth Story* is fresh in my mind I start telling her about Gram and the snot dripping into the meatloaf, and the tree surgeon suiciding himself. The words just tumble out.

Mimi is listening and putting her hand on my lap every now and then. "Oh, my Lord! Your poor grandmother!"

I nod.

She looks out the window and remains quiet for a *looong* time. Then she looks back at me, and curls her legs beneath her cute little butt. "Okay, tough guy, let's change the subject."

Mimi's Questions

Mimi keeps wanting me to talk, so she goes, "Peter, do you mind if I ask you a few personal questions? Don't worry. It'll be painless."

We are parked in the Tenakill Elementary School parking lot and I'm waiting to hear Mimi's *painless* questions. "Peter, there's no right or wrong answer to these questions…"

"They're opinional?"

"*Opinional* isn't a word, either," she says. "There's no judgment, if that's what you mean. And you don't even have to answer." *Already I'm not liking this.*

"Here goes," she says, "Which do you like best—cats or dogs?"

"Cats."

"Italian food or Chinese food?"

"Chinese."

"Hamburgers or hotdogs?"

"Hamburgers."

"A trip to France or to a trip to England?"

"England…Mimi, this is stupid."

"Yes, but I'm getting to know you better, so shut up… Pizza—thick or thin?"

"Thin."

"Romantic comedies or action films?"

"Action."

"Easy-peasy, right?" she smiles.

I nod.

"Nice hair or nice eyes?"

"Eyes."

"Okay, this is the penultimate question." She rolls her eyes. "Look at me using big words-- *penultimate* means the next to last…The Beatles or The Rolling Stones?"

"Stones."

"Blondes or brunettes?"

"Brunettes."

She claps her hands and smiles. "*Good!* Now we're getting somewhere! *I* have nice eyes and *I'm* a brunette and I *love* thin pizza!"

I narrow my eyes and go, "But c*ats* or *dogs*?"

She smiles her answer. "*CATS!* Peter, I think we're *compatible!*"

I nod. *But if Mimi knew the real me—the weak confused me deep inside—she'd jump out the car window and run home.*

"Oh!" says Mimi. "I have one last question…Did you eat it?"

"Eat what?"

"Your grandmother's snot-meatloaf?"

"I was hungry."

Hate's a Great Motivator

Tonight I'm fighting in the Felt Forum. That's a *huge* step up from high school gymnasiums. The Felt is the small arena attached to Madison Square Garden. *Small* means it seats 4,000 people.

The dressing room here is a simple concrete cubicle with a shower and a metal toilet. It's not as sophisticated as a high school classroom with books, blackboard, and a skeleton hanging in the corner. But it's one step closer to the title I'm gonna fight for.

Before the weigh-in, there's a man holding out a porkpie hat, and us four remaining middleweights are supposed to pick a number out of his hat…number 1 fights number 2…number 3 fights number 4…

I pick number 3--a guy with bulging arms, massive chest, and chiseled stomach. He looks like he was ripped from the comic book, *The Hulk*, except he's not green. His black skin is glistening with sweat as he swivels at his waist to loosen up. His long arms reach almost to the floor.

Back in the dressing room, Dom growls, "You ain't fightin' *it* till I hear *it* speak."

"You're fightin' Herb Goings?" says a trainer from the Police Athletic League, "Well, aren't you fucked!"

Herb Goings is *my father's nightmare.*

I really don't care who I fight tonight. My confidence is up. I remind myself not to fear appearances. A good physique doesn't make anyone tough. Plus, I'm no longer an unknown commodity to myself--I've scored two knockouts in two fights and have trained crazy hard with Jimmy Hargrove in the gym. My bumpy face and black eye prove it.

Tonight I feel the scream in me and I have enough hate running through my veins to make me brave.

Hate's a great motivator.

A Little Miracle

During the ref's instructions, me and Goings glare at each other from four inches. His nose is broad and flat, his lower lip is thick. His breath stinks. He's eyeballing me hard, trying to smell fear in the white boy. Black guys piss me off--they always think you're scared of them just because they're black.

It's another violent stare. Even though I hate doing it, I give in and my eyes glide over his sweaty shoulder into the crowd...I see a man sitting about eight rows back. He has a mouse-gray flattop and his hairy arms are folded across his white shirt. He's staring directly at me. ***Coach Sgro!*** The chance of that happening is 4,000 to 1! His painful football--religion was death and his sadistic practices, agonizing wind-sprints, double sessions, sweep past me.

But that's *not* the miracle! The miracle is this: When I spot Sgro I'm not flustered and my heart doesn't skip a beat. My eyes snap back to Goings.

I'm gonna kick your ass, Goings.

Fighting Herb Goings

Ding!

I'm not afraid, but my heart is beating like a bird's, quick and little. I hear the crowd murmur as one who sleeps hears.

I'm not gonna spend more than a few paragraphs explaining this fight, but it's another good one—at least for me.

I don't have to wait long before Goings attacks. His lefts and rights are curving through the air and he's grunting with each punch. He's not wasting time with jabs--he's throwing bombs. Yeah, he's hitting me a bit, and, yeah, he hits hard, but it doesn't hurt because I have a lot of bone in my skull.

THUD! One overhand right catches my jaw and I see bright pinpricks of light--but I smile—a basic lie telling him how soft he hits.

I'm digging into myself to find *jackdempsey*, and from the mud of my heart I find him. I crouch low and throw a left hook. It splats onto his face and I watch him crumble in pieces—feet, ankles, knees. As he falls, I throw a right uppercut and he completes his downward crash—trunks, body, head.

Ding!

I'm sitting on the stool, breathing hard. Dom, washing out my mouthpiece, goes, "How you feel?"

I nod okay--but I'm breathing hard. *Damn asthma.*

Ding!

Goings doesn't look so hot coming off his stool. But I'm not taking chances. He could be playing possum and sneak in a lucky punch. Boxing's a nasty sport and when people start punching each other they bleed.

I'm dancing in front of him, waiting for the prick to throw his overhand right. When he does, I counter with my left. *SPLAT!* Goings drops like a stone. *Violence is so beautiful*—it's beautiful because you master your fear despite fierce obstacles. And tonight, Goings is my fierce obstacle.

Goings isn't so beautiful when he picks himself up off the canvas.

The referee lets our fight continue, but not wisely. I drop him a third time in the last round and I sail to an easy three-round decision.

Violence is my ironic beauty.

I promised you only a few paragraphs about the fight, but I guess I got carried away. Oh, well. If you're interested in seeing this fight, look it up on the internet. It's a *doozy*--Gram's word.

Boxing Disinfects the Soul

After beating Goings, I'm prancing down the aisle heading back to my dressing room. Dom's hand is resting on the green shamrock on the back of my robe. I'm feeling good.

The crowd is buzzing with excitement. I guess they liked the way I dropped Goings three times—it was pleasantly ugly and bordering on immoral. *(Dr. Deutsch, my parents' Columbia University ally/friend would need to admit there is no **peaceful coexistence** in a boxing ring.)*

In three fights I've scored nine knockdowns. My high school friends are jumping up and down as I walk back to the dressing room. Even my teachers and coaches are attending my fights now.

I punch good.

This stutterer, bed-wetter, thumb-sucker, wart-ridden asthmatic isn't feeling like a stutterer, bed-wetter, thumb-sucker, wart-ridden asthmatic any more.

I feel like a healthy person.

I feel strangely cleansed. Within me is an inner glow, something I imagine a Catholic feels after confession. Or a wrinkled shirt feels after it's ironed.

I remember Mrs. Simon saying in English class that *Plays purify the morals.* That might be true, but boxing goes deeper—it disinfects the soul.

You're Selling Too Many Tickets

Back in the dressing room, I'm toweling off and checking my face for welts when a man opens the door. "I'm looking for Wood."

Don points his chin to me.

"Wood, you live in Closter, New Jersey?"

"No," says Dom quickly. "He lives with me in Jersey City."

"Why then are all his friends from Closter?"

"So what? He's livin' with me now."

"You realize he'll be disqualified if he lives on the south side of the Passaic River?"

"Who the hell're you?" blurts Dom.

The man points at the *Daily News* badge on his green blazer. The *Daily News* sponsors this tournament.

Dom goes, "The boy's livin' with me for the past two years. Leave us alone."

"We'll check." Then he walks out.

The thought of getting disqualified makes me inwardly exuberant, but outwardly nauseous.

"Don't worry, Pete" says Dom. "You sellin' too many tickets for 'em to throw us out. You're gonna be the middleweight champ."

Is this tournament too much pressure for me? Do I secretly want to be disqualified?

Am I not *jackdempsey* enough?

My First Childhood Memory of Dad

I'm around five years old and Dad and I are holding hands as we walk to his tiny office in the Brill Building. "Dad, what's a nigger?"

Dad stops in the middle of Broadway and yanks my arm. He's looking down at me with a serious expression—a face I'd never seen before— (except for that time when he pushed my mother to the ground.) "Never say that word," he whisper. I don't ask why, I just know that that word is bad. Dad's usually quiet and unassuming--not loud and blowhardy like my stepfather. (My stepfather is the first person who I heard say that bad word.)

To be fair, my stepfather isn't such a bad guy, he's just *not my cup of tea*—that's Dad's expression. My stepfather is arrogant, but in a polite way, if that's even possible. He might admit making a mistake but he'll never admit being wrong. Sometimes I admire his confidence and verbal ability. But he's always languaging things up with his *usual stench of words* –(that's J. D. Salinger's phrase. He's the author who wrote a really great book called **Catcher in the Rye**.)

My stepfather is an arguey lawyer, and most lawyers, as everyone knows, are basically dickheads. But honestly, if I could fight with my mouth like him I probably wouldn't be fighting with my fists.

Everyone Here Talks With Their Fists

Not sparring today--just hitting bags, skipping rope, doing pushups, sit-ups, forearm exercises, and neck bridges. Bufano's is like a small factory where muscles and self-esteem are being forged. I don't drive here to make friends. I just say is *Hi...Thanks... nice punch!...You finished hitting the bag?...See ya tomorrow.* That's about it. There's not *the usual stench of words* here in the gym. (I love that line!)

Everyone here talks with their fists. And that's just fine with me. Sometimes I think the world would be better off if people were born without a mouth. A mouth is such a small part of our bodies but it causes so much damage and so much pain.

Brian O'Melia, the sixth-ranked New Jersey heavyweight must've been watching me hit the heavy bag today because he goes, "Kid, ya don't gotta load up with each shot--each punch don't gotta be a knockout."

"Thanks," I say, dripping sweat. Then I go back doing exactly what I was doing. He means well, but he's not my coach. There are a lot of slippery sweat spots on the wooden floor around my bag, the size of nickels and quarters. All I wanna do is reach the finals and wear the Golden Gloves chain around my neck.

Bufano's Shower Stall

The shower stall in Bufano's is legendary. It's so filthy it's ridiculous. We all dread it—even Chuck Wepner and all the pros. Everyone is frightened about the germs, scabies, and ringworms lurking in there. All us tough guys tiptoe in and out like prissy ballerinas hoping we don't catch something nasty. I guess the best thing to do would be to wear rubber flip-flops, but that would admit weakness.

The thing that scares me most is the thick, cheese-like sludge on the floor. I *hate* that. I think that slippery sludge is responsible for the wicked, raw sewage smell. I kid you not.

I don't mind the flowery shower curtain encrusted with black mildew, or the slimy tiled walls, or the temperamental hot water, or even the cockroaches. It's the filthy, glutinous sludge on the concrete floor that disgusts me. And guys pissing in there. I don't like that much, either—even though I piss in there myself.

DANG! This shower stinks like rancid garbage, but what the fuck, I have to shower, don't I? Tiptoeing in gingerly and arching my back to avoid the slick shower curtain, I adjust the water temperature so it's much hotter than I really want. I do this partly for punishing myself for not working excessively hard today and partly because I don't want to indulge myself. Minor, self-induced punishment always makes me feel one-up on my competition.

Ironically, this filthy shower stall is where I'm getting clean. It's a perfect metaphor for my life.

Why Do I Have So Many Stupid Signatures?

Today I found my middle school notebooks buried beneath my *Ring* and *Boxing Illustrated* magazines and my old stamp collection. I'm flipping through the notebooks now, and embarrassed by all of my immature signatures throughout the past ten years.

1) *Peter Wood* This one shows that I have tried to master Mr. Gervin's third grade penmanship class in Hillside Elementary School

2) *Peter Woods* This one shows an 11-year-old's attempt at creativity.

3) *Peat Wood* This one shows a 14-year-old's attempt at being cool.

4) *Peter Wood* This one proves I can write my name backwards. (I do this when I'm bored in class.)

5) *Peter Wood* This one pretends I'm confident. (I read if you cross your "t" high, that means you're self-assured.)

6) *Peter Wood* This one tries to mimic Jack Dempsey's autograph.

7) *PWW* And this last one is how I sign-in before my fights.

If you remember, about 50 pages back, I said I admired my brother's handwriting—it looked so intelligent and disciplined. *Handwriting is a reflection of who we are,* says Gram. If so, why is he locked up in St. Dismas Rehabilitation Center in Hackensack recovering from heroin addiction? I hope David pulls himself together and starts living as intelligently and disciplined as his handwriting.

Mimi's Concussions

Honestly, I'm a terrible boyfriend—that's a true fact. That's because I keep banging Mimi's head--by accident--of course. She's probably suffered at least two concussions since she met me. Before you hate me, let me explain…

We were ice skating in Westwood--gliding around, hand-in-hand, when suddenly I stumbled and began to fall. Mimi tried to steady me but slipped and slammed the back of her head. *BANG!* I was surprised the *ice* didn't crack!

"YOU ASSHOLE!" she said looking up at me

We never went ice skating again.

I few weekends later Mimi and me go to the movies. She says, "Let's see *The Last Picture Show!*"

I nod

So we're driving to Tenafly, and she's wearing this floppy leather hat, and she's chattering nonstop: …*Sandy and I were smoking in the girl's bathroom when*…and *I feel sooo bad for the dying people at the nursing home*…and *I want to be a nurse one day but chemistry is so complicated*…and *My parents want to invite you over for dinner*…That's when I stop the car short while steering into a parking spot and *BANG!* -- her head slams into the windshield. She doesn't call me an *asshole* this time, even though I am. She just picks up her floppy hat from the floor, rubs her forehead, and gives me a dirty look.

Don't ask me about *The Last Picture Show* because I don't remember a damn thing.

Mimi's Third Concussion

Mimi still wants to go out with me--even after two concussions. Tonight we're wandering along a dirt path in Alpine. Actually, *I'm* walking and *she's* sitting on my shoulders.

"It's dark," she says.

"No moon."

"It's lovely being together," she coos.

"Is."

"Peter, do you like touching me?"

"Yes."

"Do you like my cute little breasts?"

"Yes."

"Are they too small?"

"They're perfect."

"Do you like when I touch *you*?"

"Yes."

"Do you like my body--*really?*"

"I *love* your body." She is wearing her black lacy panties tonight, I'm sure of it.

"Really, are my boobies too small?"

"They're perfect."

"Would you like to fuck me?"

I nod.

"I'll let you," she whispers.

"You're curfew is 10:00."

"How can you resist a hot little chic like me?"

"Mimi, your perfect little body's getting a bit heavy."

"Little me is too heavy for you?"

"I gotta put you down n-now."

"Where?"

I stop walking. "Here--on that patch of dirt."

"That's a *hole,*" she says.

"No, it's a patch of dirt."

"No! Peter, that's a hole!"

"S'not. Climb down."

"It's a *hole!*" she cries.

"I'm putting you down."

"Stop! Don't!"

Well, she was right. It *was* a hole, and her perfect little body fit perfectly into it. **BANG!** Her head hit a boulder at the bottom.

"*Dang!* I'm so sorry!"

"WHAT THE HELL IS WRONG WITH YOU?" she screams, climbing out.

"I'm a fucking asshole," I say.

So, tonight I ruined a perfectly romantic evening, but at least I got her home at 10:00.

My quarterfinals fight is in three days—I hope my head doesn't get banged as hard as Mimi's did tonight.

The Quarter Finals

Me and Dom Bufano are walking down a concrete corridor in Madison Square Garden and I notice **ABC SPORTS** printed on the side of a camera. Dom points with his chin, "You're gonna be on TV tonight."

This boxing thing is getting serious. After winning four bouts in one month, I can balance my face okay, but not my brain. Boxing on national television is scary. The quarterfinals is the time when an eighteen-year-old kid with a fragile mind gets beat.

As I walk down the corridor, I try to ignore everyone and everything by slipping my mind into a mellow neutral. I stare down at my Converse sneakers and think about *not thinking*. In a few seconds I'm thinking about me thinking about not thinking. I listen to my breath go in and out.

When we enter our dressing room, a trainer looks up and goes, "Whoa! He aint no heavyweight, is he? I don't want no heavyweight in here with my heavyweight."

Dom ignores the man, drops his dufflebag on the bench, and starts clearing a spot for me to sit. "He's a middleweight."

"Where you from?"

Dom is already rummaging around in his bag looking for the tape for my hands. "Jersey City."

"Nice place, Jersey City."

"If you're a rat," says Dom.

Some Bad News

When you're sitting in a dressing room before a fight, there aren't many things to do for fun. You can't eat Twinkies or watch cartoons. Some guys play cards and some curl up in a corner to sleep. Black guys listen to rap, Puerto Ricans it's salsa. Us whites are forced to listen to both. *Me?* I yawn and burp, and for some reason, I smell my hands. There's always a weird smell between my fingers and on the webs. Probably something germy from the gym gloves. I don't call smelling my hands *fun*, but it's something to occupy my time.

So I smell my hands and look at everyone's tattoos. My brother got **MOM & DAD** tattooed on his arm in ninth grade—the first kid to get one in our school. Me, I hate tattoos. It's a phony way to be tough or cool.

Suddenly, the door swings open. "Pete Wood in here?" It's the same Golden Gloves official as before. "How's life in *Jersey City*?" I don't like his grin. Dom and I glance at each other.

He goes, "Wood, I've got *good* news and *bad* news."

They're disqualifying me?

"The *good* news is we're letting you fight. The *bad* news is you're matched with Larry Gigliello. He snuck into this tournament just like you. He falsified his fight-card and we discovered he's a navy champ with alotta fights. But we're letting it go. Good luck, Wood." He winks his eye and walks out.

My heart starts pounding. He's the muscular dude with a navy tattoo on his bicep. I hope he doesn't break my nose like the army guy did a few years ago.

Larry Gigliello...Round 1

"I want a nice clean fight, no rabbit punches..." Six inches away, the navy cheater is breathing into my face. His eyes are ice cold but his face is slick with sweat. His hair is Vaselined into a smooth smear across his forehead like it was painted with a paintbrush. His arrogant sneer is pissing me off. It's a damn risky look--it means someone's gonna get splattered with blood very shortly.

"...and no rough stuff. This is for television, and if I..."

This cheater is chiseled muscle. Just looking at him would make most guys run back home and crawl back into bed. But if he thinks he can beat me, he's got another thing coming.

Ding!

Gigliello wades into me, winging lefts and rights, and fear flashes in my mind. *DANG!* This guy is *powerful!* Rather than back up, I crouch low—it's the safest place--with my head buried next to his blue satin trunks. His punches are whistling over head.

This prick can fight! He's hunting me down like I'm a furry little *bunny wabbit*. Most military boxers are diesel-fueled, programmed to go forward—he's no different. Throwing bombs, this bastard mauls me into a corner. I swallow a right hand as it crashes into my mouth. The audience, I hear for the first time, is screaming. I must look trapped and hurt, but I'm not. The ref, Randy Sandy, is eyeing me closely.

Eventually, I spin him and start hitting back like he's a damn sandbag but he's slugging me like *I'm* the sandbag.

Ding!

On my stool, I'm gasping for air as Dom holds the elastic waist of my trunks. "Breathe!" he says *Already* I'm tired. *Asthma sucks!* "Lateral movement!" says Dom at the ten-second buzzer.

Ding!

Round 2

The second round is—*THUD! THUD! THUD!* I can give you a bunch of beautiful details--a punch-by-punch description—but won't. What I will tell you is this: When he nails me with a good right hand, I hear crunching, like a chicken drumstick being ripped from its socket. It sounds like a broken nose. *A trophy nose.*

But I'm ripping in my punches, too. We're in a moonlit area beyond scared and it's hard to tell which one of us is more mentally ill.

THUD! THUD! THUD!

Ding!

I slump onto my stool. "Relax! Breathe!" says Dom. There's a towel over his shoulder and a Q-tip behind his ear. He's working my bloody nose and I'm struggling to fill my lungs with oxygen. I feel myself gasping for air.

Dom is all excitey. He tells me I took that round, but we need one more.

I blink my eyes *"Yes"* but my lungs are screaming *"No!"*

Dom lifts me off the stool by my armpits. "You can take this guy! You been sparrin' Hargrove and he sparred Sonny Liston!" Don's grasping for logic like I'm gasping for air.

Ding!

Round 3

The navy cheater meets me center ring and we start plugging. Don't give me this shit about blood clots or anything—I don't care. Neither does he. His cocky face looks like raw meat. I have never hit a guy harder, but he keeps coming. I'm getting hit good, too, but what the fuck, I got this far, I refuse to lie down or quit. My mind is still in that moonlit area.

By the end of the round, I've landed so many left hooks, I can't hold up my left arm anymore. I feel 99 percent dead, but a thick-skinned stupidity keeps me going. I'm digging down deep, trying to coax out the furry figure that swings from branch to branch in the back of my brain. By now, my punches are limp, and my ribs are heaving with exhaustion. Flesh is burning away, melting in hot sweat drops. My brother is killing himself with heroin—I'm killing myself with punching.

I claw down deep and drag one more exhausted fist through the air. It splats onto his face.

DING!

The referee, Gigliello, and me are standing in the middle of the ring waiting for the decision to be announced. I close my eyes, cover my face with my glove, and pray. *Please, God, please…*

"*The Winner is…Wood!*"

I turn to Gigliello and pant, "Goofigh."

"Good fight," he goes.

I don't give a damn if it sounds corny, but that's the beauty of boxing—a rugged three round fight makes two complete strangers very much the same—*tired*—and their souls kinda touch in the ring. That's why you see fighters hug after a fight—I saw in Giglielo the toughness, courage, and skill that might also be in me.

195

After the fight, I drop into a chair. Gigliello has pushed me someplace I never knew I had. After they walk me back to the dressing room, I start puking but nothing comes out.

I wonder if Jack Dempsey ever puked after a fight.

"Get a doctor!" hollers Dom.

The Next Morning

My head's throbbing like a bad tooth. The skin under both eyes and on the bridge of my nose is red, black and blue. But the worst are my jaw muscles because I can't open my mouth. I remember when a black eye was something to brag about. I remember my thrilling childhood visions of Jack Dempsey, broken-nosed glory, flat-nosed manhood, and all that crap. I had *wanted* this. But now I'm beginning to understand that's all a childish illusion. Fighting is delightful only to those who have never experienced it.

My mother is standing in the doorway with her hand pressed to her lips. "Oh, Sweetie! Look at you!" She's dressed in her elegant Fifth Avenue suit and her auburn hair is perfectly spun glass.

She tries to touch my left eye. "Don't pet me," I say.

"Look at your eyes! I've spent so much time running after you and David making sure you both were safe. And now you're letting complete strangers knock you on your head."

"I won," I say proudly. For some reason, I feel danger because I might be wanting something back from her...w*hat*, I'm not sure.

Gram enters the room.

"Look at my son's face!" says my mother.

"That's the Irish in him," says Gram. "I'll get an ice-pack."

The Next Day at School

Here is a quick sampling of comments from students and teachers when they see me today.

In Homeroom:

Holy cow! Look at your face! says Mrs. Horwin, the school nurse.

I go, "Yeah, well, you should see the other guy." It's a corny line, but it gets chuckles from the class.

Period 1:

Crow, my sparring partner, says, *"Man, you were great last night!"*

"You were there?"

"Yeah—me, Squirrel, Abe, Beddoe, Frankie, Jack—all us guys !"

"How'd I l-look?"

"Tough as crabgrass! But I still can kick your boney ass!"

Period 2:

Our tiny principal, Mr. Colantoni, walks in after class and says, *"I remember you as a little stuttering freshman, and then last night I'm watching you fight in The Felt Forum. I mean who is this strange student called Peter Wood?"*

Period 3:

In study hall, brainiac Gary Peterson says, *"I remember when you stood in the ocean and punched the waves in Lavallette? Well, this is a dumb question, but what's it like to hit a real person?"*

"Feels good."

"What're you thinking when you're hitting him?"

"Not much. I'm just punching."

Period 4:

In gym, Coach Mott says, I'm not a boxing fan, but last night you showed our school a lot of heart and guts and another part of the anatomy."

"Balls?"

"As your baseball coach I can't say 'balls'."

Period 5:

Mrs. Simon, my favorite teacher says, *"When I watched you last night, you reminded me of me."*

"Really?"

"When I was seven years old, I remember looking into a microscope at a slide of water, which I thought was clean and pure. I told my mother, 'Look! It has wiggles!' She said, 'Yes--impurities.' Well, last night, I was watching you and I spotted wiggles."

"Wiggles?"

"Yes--in your motivation. It's obvious you won, but the most important things in life are hidden—like water under a microscope. Peter, what is your motivation? Why are you boxing?"

"It's fun."

"You're full of shit."

"I like b-boxing."

"Hitting someone?"

"Yeah."

"Peter, you're a wonderful student and have a way with words, but you're emotionally blind. Don't you realize athletically you're boxing—emotionally you're crying?"

I look at her--why is my favoritest teacher being such a bitch?

"Peter, don't you realize who your real opponent was last night...yourself."

Period 6:

Coach Sgro stops me near the cafeteria, gives me a hard obnoxious handshake, and says, *"Nice fight. Proud a you."*

"Coach, I wouldn't be winning these fights if it weren't for you."

He seems embarrassed and goes, *"You ready for your next fight?"*

"I think so."

"Think so? I didn't teach you "I think so.""

"Yeah, I'm ready."

"When is it?"

"Next week."

Then he swings around and shoulder-blocks me into a locker. *"Be alert! Always be alert!"* Then he walks away. Coach still treats me like dirt. That's okay. I've learned to thrive on my healthy sense of inadequacy.

Period 7:

Mimi hands me today's *Daily News* and points to Jack Smith's article. She says, *"Read where my father highlighted in red."*

"Contenders from three divisions clambered into the ring and belted away. All winners will go on to the semifinals and are one step closer

to the last stop at Madison Square Garden...Sharing the plaudits of the fans...was Jersey City's Peter Wood from Bufano's Gym, a contender for the 160 Sub-Novice diadem. Wood and Mike Gigliello, a conveyor-belt installer from the Bayonne P.A.L., staged one of the most thrilling slugfests of the campaign with Wood taking a slender decision after three furious rounds."

Period 8:

I walk up one flight of noise to math. Like I said, whoever invented math should be shot. I'm eighteen years old and I still secretly count on my fingers... 8+5 and 7+ 6 just haven't clicked yet.

As I walk into math class, Mr. Buffington looks at me and says, *Golly! Look at your face!*

It occurs to me as I read this chapter that I crave attention and risk brain damage to get it. That's a bit pathetic, if you ask me. Am I still trying to get back my *Peter Wood Fan Club*?

My Mother

Don't listen to me when I say *I hate my mother's guts.* Honestly, I might not *really* hate her, but I don't like her much. I have never allowed her to go to my football games or watch my fights. I just don't want her there. She'd be so out of place and I'd be so embarrassed. Who wants their pretty perfumed mother crying at a prizefight?

In fairness, I've been unfair to my mom because every single day since she left my father, she's worked nonstop and has blossomed into a successful clothing designer. She's gone from sweatshop worker to a successful designer at Kaiser-Roth on 51st Street and 5th Avenue. *(The First Lady, Betty Ford, even wrote my mother a letter on official White House stationery saying "I love your original tri-colored robe!)*

Yeah, I should be proud of her accomplishments, but, honestly, it's hard to forgive a mother who leaves for New York City every morning and leaves her suffering family behind—like she left my dad. But I realize it's not only her who's been doing the leaving—it's me, as too.

In my sophomore English class, Mrs. Simon always repeated her favorite Mark Twain quote: **Forgiveness is the fragrance the violet sheds on the heel that has crushed it.** I wrote it in my notebook and think about it all the time because it relates to me.

Yeah, forgiveness is a good thing, but I just can't seem to get there yet.

Turning Bufano's Upside Down

Five months ago when I started training in Bufano's my sweat smelled like McDonald's hamburgers, sausage pizza, and Hostess cupcakes. But now, I kid you not, my sweat smells almost sweet.

I'm humbled that I'm even surviving in here. It's a gym full of grunting and groaning, shouting, cursing, slapping of jump ropes, and pounding of bags. I bet if you turned Bufano's upside down and shook it, a shitload of anger, hostility, bitterness, neurosis, weird fixations, pathological distrust, inferiority complexes, hang-ups, anti-social paranoia would tumble out. That's the exact same with my high school cafeteria. There's alotta of mental health issues in there, too. If you turned it upside down and shook it, the same anger, fear, hostility, bitterness, neurosis, weird fixations, pathological distrust, inferiority complexes, hang-ups, anti-social paranoia would tumble out.

Bufano's is crawling with disadvantaged men and twisted souls who are more dirt poor than filthy rich. I once read *the biggest disadvantage of being poor is not having enough money to afford psychoanalysis.* I think that line was meant to be funny, but when you think about it, really think about it, it's sad.

Today when I walked up the stairs to train, as always there was a lump in my throat…but two amazing things happened:

Firstly—I almost knocked out Jimmy Hargrove with a left hook! After three rounds, I tapped *him* on top of *his* headgear and said, "Good job, Jimmy!"

Secondly--After Kenny Warner, a pro middleweight, watched me spar, he says, "Pete, you and Earl "The Pearl" Monroe got the quickest reflexes I ever seen." *(Monroe is a pro basketball player for the Knicks.)*

"Wow! Thanks, Kenny!"

I love this gym! No one in here might not know much about Emily Post etiquette, or courtesy flushes, or flossing their teeth--but there's still a great amount of etiquette and decorum in here. No one struts around being an asshole. And there's no racial crap here. The only color in Bufano's is the *red* corner and the *blue* corner.

Bad to the Bone

Bufano's Gym is a living and breathing George Bellows painting full of dark shadows, interesting characters, and drama. That's why the rock singer, George Thorogood, used Bufano's, (and its attached pool hall), for the backdrop of his music video *Bad to the Bone*. Bo Diddley, the blues/rock 'n roll songwriter and Willie Mosconi, the legendary billiard champion, are both in it--along with Dom Bufano, and a young, gum-chewing strumpet.

A little known fact: George Thorogood, like me, is a stutterer. He wrote *Bad to the Bone* in response to bullies picking on him because of his speech impediment. In the song, Thorogood purposely stammers over his Bs.

I'm b-b-b-ad to the b-b-b-one

If I had my way, his song would be the national anthem for all us stutterers. (Along with *My Generation* by The Who, of course.)

The Semifinals

I woke up this morning with a wicked sore throat. Tonight's the semifinals and I'm getting sick? *Dang!* Why am I putting myself through all this boxing crap? Why can't I just lead a normal life like all of the other students at my school?

Because I wanna discover the *jack-dempsey* inside me. That's why.

Ever since entering this stupid tournament, I've had four months of liquid shits and haven't banged Mimi. And I haven't pulled myself off even once. My miserable little cock keeps gulping back wet dreams.

*****

Dom and I are driving to my fight through the Holland Tunnel where the trapped air smells like the dead air inside a basketball. My throat is getting worse, but I don't wanna tell Dom. What good would it do?

Dom says he wants to turn me pro after The Gloves. "There's alotta money in boxing for a tough kid like you."

"I'll think about it," I go.

Dom turns north, up Tenth Avenue, past brick warehouses and abandoned buildings. It's a cold March night and a group of whores are standing practically naked on the corner. *Why do women wanna become whores?*

Why do men wanna become pro fighters?

As we drive closer to The Garden, my throat is getting worse and I'm kinda hoping Dom gets us into a car accident so I won't have to fight.

*****

Standing at the weigh-in are us four surviving middleweights ready to find out who's gonna fight who. A Golden Gloves official calls out, "Alexis Griffith?"

"Here." It's an angry ugly voice.

"Jose Ventura?"

"Here." It's a quiet murmur.

"Walter Johnson...or is it *Johnston*?"

"Don't matter--both're slave names." It's a nasty chip-on-the-shoulder voice.

"Pete Wood?"

I nod.

The official is holding his porkpie hat and goes, "Boys, in case you forgot, I'll explain the procedure again. Each fighter takes a number outta this hat. Number 1 fights number 2. Number 3 fights number 4. Got it?"

I reach in and pick *Johnston* or *Johnson*. He stands 6'2", but his afro makes him 6'6". He starts glaring down at me. "Good luck, Woody," he says. "I'll tell the ref to have a basket ready at ringside to catch your head when I knock it off."

Eating Vasoline

Okay—I'll try to keep this chapter short.

Johnson, (or *Johnston,*) is gnawing his mouthpiece during instructions. This kid *definitely* has anger-management problems. Is he angry because I beat Herb Goings, his NYC Rec stablemate, or because I look like a white person--which I am?

Clang!

Johnson whips out three *looong* jabs—each a bull's eye on my nose—and already I'm tasting blood. I crouch low and punches bounce off the top of my head, but he snakes in a nice straight right which I take on my eye. Another *looong* jab spears me and I see a black-blue-red-green colored color. He's beating my ass good.

He muscles me against the ropes and I clinch. *You're sick, Pete! Lay down! You shouldn't even be here in a ring…where is the jack-dempsey in me?*

"Break!" barks the referee.

We step back.

"Box!"

I step in low, dig into the canvas, and with a grunt, I come up with a slashing left hook—it's the best fucking punch in the history of my life. It lands with a mushy thud. One second Johnson is standing there, then, ***Poof!*** he's lying on the canvas. The shot was a solid piece of hope—a tire-iron knocking his jaw into his throat. It was a collision that I'd often dreamt about and Johnson had nightmares over.

I knock him out in 41 seconds.

I've reached the Golden Gloves finals…but I'm disgusted with myself because for a split second, I wanted to pussy out.

✳✳✳✳✳

Back in the dressing room, Dom is talking while I'm putting on my socks. I'm not listening, but I hear him anyway.

"*Jeez, Pete!* You punched his fuckin' ear into his brain! After you win the finals next week, I'll turn you pro. We'll go slow at first, then pick up momentum. When you hit people they go *down*!"

I look at him and say nothing.

"You got *The Calling* in you, boy!"

"Like a priest?"

"Exactly! They're pissing in their pants when they fight you."

I nod.

"Al Certo has been sniffing around the gym. He's interested in handling you."

I look up. "The pro manager?" He nods.

I rub my throat. "Dom, I don't feel so g-good…sore throat."

He digs into his bag and pulls out a jar of Vasoline, hands it to me, and says, "Swallow a spoonful before you go to bed, and then again in the morning when you wake up."

Eat Vasoline?

I'll Be Fine

I can blame this whole damn chapter on Larry Gigliello who I beat in the quarterfinals--the navy cheater who drained me so dry I couldn't walk back to my dressing room--and when I got there I started puking.

He's why I'm lying here in bed, sick with the flu. *He's why* I haven't done roadwork or trained in seven days. *He's why* I'm coughing up phlegm that looks like butter scotch pudding. *He's why* I can't eat solid food because my throat's *killing* me.

Dang! My next fight's four days away and my body feels like a sick piece of poultry. At the dinner table, the only thing I can swallow are Gram's mashed potatoes with extra butter.

"Oh, dear!" says my mother watching me cringe as I swallow.

"I'll be fine," I wheeze. I start coughing up more phlegm and hawk it into my napkin.

Gram asks, "What did Dr. Nagel say this afternoon?"

"Rest and fluids."

"Are you're taking antibiotics?" my mother asks.

Mr. Schizza goes, "You still have a few more days to recover."

I nod.

"By the way," he adds, "the men at the White Beaches Golf Club are placing bets on you—Yogi Berra plunked down $25."

Sally goes, "Everybody in school's rooting for you. We're all going! Jack Klie even hired a bus."

*****

Back in bed, I'm wearing the thermal underwear my dad bought me years ago. I close my eyes and start thinking. When I get through thinking about the stuff I wanna think about, I start thinking about the stuff I *don't* wanna think about—like Yogi Berra betting on me and a busload of friends. Don't they know my lungs are full of snot? Hey! I got a brilliant idea! I should bring a snot bucket to school for **Show 'n Tell!** It'll be great! Then everyone will see I'm sick!

I close my eyes and hear Dom yelling: *Where's Pete! I bust my ass to get him to Madison Square Garden and now he doesn't come to the gym!* Maybe I should bring the snot bucket to Bufano's?

*****

Last night, my dad called and said, *"Peter, yesterday I ate lunch at Jack Dempsey's restaurant. Jack sat down with me and said he's been following you in the Daily News. He wants to meet you."*

Jack Dempsey!... Jack Dempsey!... Jack Dempsey!

People! Don't you understand it?... I'm sick?

Right then it hits me hard…I know what I gotta do…

The Day Before My Fight

I walk up the staircase, through the pool hall, and into the gym.

"Fine fuckin' time to get sick," blurts Dom. Then he adds, "Hargrove won last night—so you're both in the finals."

The day before a fight, I should be resting but Dom puts me in with Johnny Sullivan, a pro welterweight.

*****

After suiting up, I walk back onto the floor and watch Chuck Wepner and Brian O'Melia slug it out for three rounds. After Wepner takes off his headgear, his sweaty face looks pink and soft and his skin looks like it could be spread with a butter knife, I kid you not.

(By the way--a month ago I broke Brian O'Melia's nose while sparring. We sparred the next day and he wore a catcher's mask...Four years later, Wepner fought Muhammad Ali for the heavyweight title. So that means this: I punched the nose of Brian O'Melia who punched the nose of Chuck Wepner who punched the nose of Muhammad Ali. I'm just vain enough to tell you this.)

Well, anyway, I love fighters. Chuck Wepner Brian O'Melia, and Jimmy Hargrove. I can list ten pages of fighters I admire: Ismael Laguna, Emile Griffith, Joe Louis, Rocky Marciano, Sugar Ray Robinson, Mickey Walker, Willie Pep, Carlos Monzon, Dick Tiger... Fighters are the gutsiest people in the whole wide world. But if Dom is right about me--that I have a *Calling* to be a fighter--then he is a poor judge of character and God is a dangerous maniac.

*****

In the corner of my eye I see Al Certo the hot-shot boxing manager. He and two business-suity types are eyeing me. Blood begins pounding in my ears, my lips are parched, and my nose is sore from sneezing.

212

Dom is sticking my hand into a 16-ounce glove, still sweaty from Wepner. "Box good. Certo's watchin'."

Well, I have something else planned...

Pete—You Shouldn't a Done It

Sullivan and me are up in the ring circling each other...now he's throwing out quick stinging jabs...

...**Monkey Mind** whispers: *No, Pete! Don't do it!....*

...Certo is evaluating me...

...**Monkey Mind** whispers: *No, Pete! Don't do it!...*

...I'm bulling Sullivan onto the ropes, banging a few body shots, and shuffling back...

...**Monkey Mind** whispers: *No, Pete! Don't do it!....*

...I'm inching out my chin and waiting...

...**Monkey Mind** whispers: *No, Pete! Don't do it!...*

...I know I can time Sullivan perfectly. When he throws his right, I'll roll with his punch, drop to the canvas...*Hey, it's like bringing in a snot bucket and explaining I'm sick...,,,*

,,,...I'm lying on the canvas and Sullivan is now helping me to my feet. "Hey! I hardly touched you!" he says.

*****

Now I'm taking a shower in the dirty stall and feeling great shame...and relief...the damage is done...I've introduced myself to myself...I've learned a very painful life-lesson: **Either the world is too strong for me, or I'm too weak for it.**

Monkey Mind whispers: *Pete—there's no Jack Dempsey in you.*

The Golden Gloves Finals

"We made it, brother," smiles Jimmy. I smile back at him, but whenever I'm called 'brother' I cringe. Being a brother hasn't been fun—but, yeah, we did make it—we're now sitting in a Madison Square Garden dressing room. *This is the big juicy status I've worked so hard for. A Golden Gloves title is serious stuff.*

"Pete, you're gonna be fine," says Dom, although his face says otherwise. Earlier this morning when I stepped onto the scale, we discovered a **big** problem--I had dropped six pounds--a whole weight class in a week. That's because I didn't wanna eat much since I wasn't training, and didn't wanna come in over-weight and lose the fight on the scale. After the weight-in Dom rushed me to Tad's Steakhouse for a steak, a baked potato, and broccoli.

"Yeah, you'll be fine," he goes, patting my knee.

*****

I'm sitting here--but *toooo* relaxed. My opponent, Jose Ventura, doesn't scare me—he's a runner. I've beaten much better guys. There's only one thing that is bothering me: ***Can I go the distance...Will I run out of gas?***

The People in My Head

I'm closing my eyes and seeing people who aren't there. My stepfather is saying...*Yogi Berra has $25 riding on you.*

Coach Sgro is saying...*I'll be in sitting there in Madison Square rooting for you.*

Squirrel is saying...*Bite the bastard's shoulder—thumb his eye.*

Crow is saying...*Hands up--chin down!*

My father is saying....*Jack Dempsey wishes you good luck. He wants to meet you.*

Mimi is saying...*Don't let him hit you below the belt.*

Gram is kissing my forehead at the front door, saying...*Peter, think positive thoughts. You can achieve anything if you believe in yourself.*

Mrs. Simon is saying...*Peter, your opponent is yourself.*

My mother is saying...*Oh, Honey...*

My brother, David, wrote a letter from St. Dismus Rehabilitation Center in Hackensack:

> *I read in the* **Daily News** *this creep wants to kick my baby brother's butt.*

> *I'm counting on you to be strong. All us guys in here—even the Ricans—are rooting for you. Sorry I can't be there to cheer you on. – Love, Dave*

His handwriting is still good.

There Aint No Sense Worryin'

A Golden Gloves official calls out, *"Vito Antuofermo!"* A welterweight with a trophy nose and a lot of facial bruises stands up, crosses himself, and exits. *(Eight years later, he will become the undisputed middleweight champion of the world.)*

Dom looks at Jimmy and me and says, "Remember, boys—tonight's just other fight—don't get nervous."

Jimmy goes, "Dom, there aint no sense worryin' 'bout things we got control over, because if we got control over 'em, there aint no sense worryin'. And there aint no sense worryin' 'bout things we *don't* got control over, 'cause if we don't got control over 'em, there aint no sense worryin'."

Dom looks at me and shrugs.

"Yeah," says Jimmy, "only a few million people watchin' tonight."

I close my eyes and listen to something squishing in Jimmy's stomach.

"Pepsi," he grins.

Shut Up, Hargrove

"Eddie Gregory, you're up!" Gregory exits yawning. *(Nine years later, Eddie changed his name to Mustapha Muhammad, and became the undisputed light-heavyweight champion of the world.)*

I yawn. I burp.

Jimmy looks at me and whispers, "Is it true what the guys in the gym say about you?"

I look up.

Dom snaps, "Shut up, Hargrove--mind your own business." He then tosses Jimmy tonight's fight program. Jimmy starts looking at the photos of tonight's 36 finalists—flyweights to heavyweights. "Jus' look at all these minimum-wage boys! They look like they live inside a garbage can."

I slide over to look. These are the toughest bastards in New York City, and my picture is here with them. I point to Jimmy's opponent, William Stewart, a dude who looks like he's capable of inflicting great pain.

Jimmy points to Jose Ventura, a guy with lopsided nostrils and a wobbly afro. "There be yours." Jimmy then points to a featherweight. "This guy probably deals drugs."

"My brother's a drug addict."

Jimmy looks at me.

"He shoot?"

I nod. "He's in rehab now."

Jimmy pats my knee. "Hope he cleans up, brother."

To pass time, I look at my photo. I may look tough, but inside I'm wall-to-wall carpeting, and big soft pillows. That's why I'm so proud to be with these guys tonight. In a weird way, we are the sane ones. There's more violence—verbal, psychological, political, sexual, social, and racial—*outside* the ring than in it. Fighters, in a strange way, are *one with Nature*. If only I could actually believe those last three sentences.

The door opens. "Leroy Jones—you're up!" All 250 pounds of him lumbers out the door. *(In 1978, Jones won the NABF heavyweight championship against "Hercules" Mike Weaver. In 1980, he fought for the WBC heavyweight title, losing to Larry Holmes.)*

I'm waiting for my name to be called…

Wood! You're On!

"Wood! You're on!"

I walk to the toilet, pull down my cup and blue satin trunks and squeeze out one last drop. When you're wearing 12-ounce gloves, it's not as easy as it sounds, and I piss all over my leg.

"Let's go," says Dom, holding the water bucket.

Jimmy slaps my back "Be cool, bro'!"

I'm walking to the ring…*six pounds lighter…can I last three rounds? Will I run outta gas?*

The Fight

...a packed Garden of 24,000 fans...bright spot-lights...TV cameras...I'm in the blue corner, swinging my arms apelike...Ventura is in the gold corner bouncing up and down.

During instructions, Ventura is grinning. "Hey, Pete—you be six pounds lighter tonight."

I'm staring back. "Fuck you, Ventura. I'm knocking you out tonight."

"Aint happenin'."

"Happenin'."

"Pete, you got asthma, you suck your thumb, you have warts, and you wet your bed."

Of course this conversation never happened—it's monkey mind...I walk back to my corner and say, "Dom, I hope..."

"You will! You will!" he says, jamming in my mouthpiece.

I have another secret plan...

DING!

Ventura is circling right--his jab is licking the air around my face--*fear jabs.* I slip inside and bang his belly but he ties me up easily. Close to his mouth I smell eggs.

The ref breaks us.

Ventura continues moving right--he knows my left hook will break his skull.

His jabs are missing because I'm swiveling my neck—no excess movement—no ducking, parrying, or sidestepping—just **conserving**

energy...*That's my secret plan: Conserve energy--coast in round one, and take the last two.*

Half-heartedly, I bull him onto the ropes and clinch. He dances away and lands a nice right. In the middle of the ring, he flurries and I hold on. Toward the end of the round, I realize while I'm conserving energy. He's doing something--*punching*.

DING!

"Get with it!" hollers Dom.

"Tired."

"I don't care! Fight!"

I'm sucking in air...blowing it out...sucking it in...blowing it out...sucking it in...

DING!

Ventura has grown confident, stepping in with jabs and straight right hands. I crank out my left hook but he slides away gracefully. I rush in, but he has good footwork and switches directions. It's like I'm debating my stepfather who sidesteps and glides away with clever words.

My brilliant plan of conserving energy is backfiring. Ventura is starting to think he can actually beat me! He steps in with a fast one-two. Blood is dripping from my nose. I try to get angry, but can't. I'm losing this fight.

DING!

The Last Round

When I reach the corner, Dom doesn't have the stool ready, so I squat on the lower rope and my butt almost hits the canvas. Have you ever heard 24 thousand people go **"OOOHHH!"** all at once?

Dom's now wiping blood off my face with a wet sponge. "You're losin' it--you gotta take this round!"

DING!

I run across the ring without grace, skill, or worry. *This is the last round.*

I'm trying to trap Ventura onto the ropes, but the bastard flits away. I finally catch him and begin slamming lefts and rights. He's clinching now, and accidentally-on-purpose, my left hook strays below his belt. The crowd is glued to the violence. I'm *joe-fraziering* forward looking to land my left. I'm punching like an exhausted madman.

DING!

Dom hugs me in the corner. "Proud of ya, son," he says.

"D' I win?"

"We'll see."

The Decision

Flood lights funnel into the middle of the ring...the announcer taps his mic... *"The Winner of the Sub-Novice Middleweight Division is...Ventura!...Ventura!"*

Ashamed and humiliated, I hunch through the ropes, walk down the steps, and plod down the aisle back to the dressing room. *You horseshit! You blew it!* That's when a man who looks a lot like Perry Mason--a man who said *mankind, by its very nature, is bad,* a man who bought me a set of boxing gloves and an Everlast heavybag, a man who brought me to my first amateur fight—strides up to me and says, "Good fight, Pete!"

"FUCK YOU!" I scream, and skulk into the tunnel back to the dressing room.

*****

In the dressing room, Dom kicks a burnt-out butt on the floor and tosses a towel in the air. "Just 'cause we're from Jersey, they robbed us!" I can tell he wants to punch the wall but can't because Jimmy fights next.

I'm sitting here for two minutes...three minutes...four minutes, toeing the dead butt. *Fuck me. I always screw things up in the end.* After my pity-party, I step into the shower and start banging my head on the wall.

"Hey, you okay in there?" yells a voice. There's no harm in a loser like me banging his head on a wall, is there?

"Stop it!" yells the voice.

I guess my pity-party isn't quite over because I start replaying the fight. **Fuck Me!** Then I start replaying my ten-year boxing journey. It's like I'm looking at myself through a rearview mirror and realizing boxing's been a minor suicide. My mind's become a living corpse.

Fighting has dulled me mentally and has twisted me into someone else. It's like I've buried my own mirror. *Dang!* It took thousands of rounds of fighting and sparring for me to write this paragraph.

Suddenly, I hear Gram yell...*Peter! Wake up and fly right!*...

She's absolutely right—and I pivot. This sport *is* crazy, but it's a *beautiful* crazy. Boxing's been a *blessing*. It's allowed me to *explode-
-not implode*, like someone else I know. It's detoxed me—I've puked out poison by punching, and it has proven a softy like me ain't so soft. I guess I needed to figure that out the hard way. Yeah, boxing was misery and happiness rolled up in one. Boxing is a healthy sickness. *Dang!* It took me *another* thousand rounds of fighting to write *that* paragraph.

I've finally stopped banging my head and water is pouring down my body...My dad always said *A beautiful melody is always waiting to be discovered*... Well, tonight, I discovered my place of discovery was the ring.

...and I apologize for saying *fuck you* to my stepfather.

The Golden Gloves Necklace

After getting dressed, I walk into the office to pick up *the one thing* that proves I'm not just another ordinary kid—*the one thing* that proves it's all been worthwhile—*the Golden Gloves necklace—except it's silver.* An official hands me a beautiful silver chain with a boxing glove pendant studded with a ruby. "Here you go, Wood." *The winner gets gold with a diamond.*

I clip it around my neck and look at myself in the mirror.

"Back next year, Wood?" asks the official.

"Maybe."

"We hope so—you're one helluva fighter."

I walk down the hallway and I know the truth--I will *not* return next year. I'm tired of this obsession. I never loved fighting...*I worshipped it.* I threw myself into this crazy sport with passion—it was fire and magic.

Yeah, I've paid a high price for this necklace, but I'd do it again in a heartbeat. Boxing has shaped me in a good way and has kept me from becoming *really* lost. Entering the Gloves has been a priceless morsel of life. It's been ten years of angst, but that's *totally* okay. (*Angst* is another good word I learned in Mrs. Simon's class. It means, *a feeling of anxiety, apprehension, or insecurity.*)

The truth is I *never* was just an ordinary kid...and my opponent has always been myself.

Boxing's been the dark eyeglasses that I did not see when I looked through them. (*Hey, that's pretty damn poetic. Mrs. Simon would be proud!*)

What Do the Guys in the Gym Say About Me?

Jimmy, Coach, and I are walking down 29th, and the white bandage over Jimmy's eye is grabbing people's attention. Dom is all, "They robbed both a youse."

"S'all right," says Jimmy. "Next year."

We stop at the corner and wait for the light. Dom frowns while touching his bad eye and says, "The bad thing about life is that it's very real."

As we walk across 9th, no one's saying much, except Jimmy who's humming *My Girl*. When we reach Dom's car, I say, "Jimmy, what do the guys in the gym say about me?"

Dom begins shaking his head.

"Nah, man, nothin'," goes Jimmy.

"C'mon, tell me."

Dom is still shaking his head.

I drop my duffle bag to the sidewalk. "Dom, I aint getting in the car until Jimmy tells me."

"Shut up, Jimmy," says Dom.

"Tell me, or I'm walking home."

Jimmy shrugs. "Well, the guys be sayin' you once lived in, ya know…"

"Shut up, Jimmy!"

"In what?" I go.

"A nuthouse…a mental institution."

I think about existing for ten years in a house I never wanted to be in.

"Did ya?"

"…Nah, it was more of a three-ring circus."

*****

Driving back to New Jersey through the Holland Tunnel, I'm thinking about the Schizza circus and how I'll be moving out in a few months.

"Must be fun livin' in a circus."

"Well, you learn a lot about peaceful coexistence." Then I say, "Did I ever tell you my father is a songwriter? The Mills Brothers and Tony Bennett sang his songs on the *Tonight Show.*"

"No shit."

I start singing *The Little Boy. (You'll find the lyrics on page 2.)*

Jimmy laughs. "Yo, bro', you *is* crazy!"

"Maybe." But I know I'm not. For the first time in years I feel free— somehow I've hatched.

I finger my silver necklace proudly—it's not gold, but that's okay. If I can reach the Golden Gloves finals, I can reach the finals anywhere. There will be other dreams and battles but nothing to do with boxing. What my future dreams and battles will be, I don't know.

But I do know this…This Saturday I'm meeting Jack Dempsey! Dad and I are driving into the city to eat lunch with Mr. Dempsey at his restaurant. Dad says Mr. Dempsey has the best cheesecake.

The End

Acknowledgments

If writing is so solitary. Why are there so many people to thank?

Like its author, this book has been rescued many times by extraordinary proof-readers, editors, and friends. I thank them for their support and belief in me: Sharon Ezzeldin, Cynthia Pierce, Grazyna Anstett, Grace Dupree, Robert Mladinich, and the irrepressible Hollywood actor, Michael C. Gwynne.

I am indebted to the entire staff at Saw Mill Athletic Club East, especially Bea Jazz, for her unwavering buoyancy, laughter, and professionalism.

A profound and heartfelt thank you to neurosurgeon David Gordon and the neurological staff at Phelps Hospital who made it possible for me to sit down and write the final pages of this book.

My thanks, my love.

Printed in the USA
CPSIA information can be obtained
at www.ICGtesting.com
LVHW061108121223
766302LV00020B/876